# COSTUME

## The Journal of the Costume Society

Volume 46, Number 2

*A Volume for the London Olympics*

Produced by Maney Publishing
for the Costume Society

2012

# Contents

Selected content is available online free of charge at
www.ingentaconnect.com/content/maney
To sign up for free tables of contents alerts please see
**www.maney.co.uk**/online/tocs

*Costume*, vol. 46, no. 2, 2012

# Editorial (1)

The staging of the Olympic Games in the UK this year gives us the opportunity to think about the clothes and appearance of those who take part in sporting activities. You may not be a great fan of sport yourself but you will see from the *Costume* archive just how much interest there has been over the years in dress for sports of all kinds and across many periods. Pat Poppy has compiled a checklist from the Journal's back numbers of articles about sports clothing and we present this to our readers on page 235 of this themed issue.

As the first of our special issues devoted to one subject, we have looked beyond the strict confines of dress history scholarship and embraced contributions from the fields of social sciences and sports studies. *Costume* readers will be aware that this is not our usual fare. The Editors feel it is important to give other voices a chance to talk about dress, and an opportunity arose to collaborate with Professor John Hughson following a workshop organized by him and devoted to sports dress held at the University of Central Lancashire in the autumn of 2011. In this Olympic year, we decided to give over the June issue to some of the papers presented at that workshop and we trust that scholars and curators from different disciplines will find things to learn from each other. It has been a pleasure working with Professor Hughson, who introduces the essays in more detail overleaf.

In addition to the essays and the archival list, we are also able to offer a selection of images, new to most of our readers, of extant sports garments and photographs from UK collections. An actual garment often speaks volumes, and these photographs will surely stimulate questions and make us reflect on the experience of wearing such clothes and the effect they might produce.

We are very pleased to welcome Anna Buruma as our compiler of the New and Recent Books List. She takes over from James Snowden and has done sterling work with a very short deadline. Christine Stevens, our Reviews Editor, has likewise come up with a good number of book reviews in a short interval as we move over to two issues a year.

We include an obituary of Monsignor Richard Rutt CBE (affectionately known to some readers as the 'Knitting Bishop') who, in a small but significant way, made a contribution to the history of sportswear in the pages of this Journal. It is also with great regret that we report the death of Katrina Honeyman (1950–2011), Professor of Social and Economic History at the University of Leeds, whose innovative studies of the Leeds tailoring industries will be well known to our readers. She supported the Pasold Research Fund (which promotes research into the economic and social history of textiles) for many years and in several ways, publishing two books in the Pasold series and serving as a distinguished editor of the journal *Textile History*.

PENELOPE BYRDE AND VERITY WILSON

   DOI: 10.1179/174963012X13319136517034

*Costume*, vol. 46, no. 2, 2012

# Editorial (2)

In the year of London hosting the Games of the XXXth Olympiad, it is appropriate that this special issue of *Costume* dealing with sports-related clothing commences with an Olympic-related paper. Jean Williams presents a study of Olympic swimming costumes, specifically the racing swimsuit worn by Britain's first women's medal-winning swimmer, Jennie Fletcher, at the 1912 Games. Fletcher's costume, revealing for the time, represented a radical departure from the normal modesty constrictions applicable to women's swimwear. Thus, Williams contends, technology, servicing sport performance as an almost scientific pursuit, prevailed over the customary social nervousness associated with women exposing their flesh in public. Fletcher's working-class and Leicester background is made relevant to the analysis.

In the following paper, Fiona Skillen examines the contradictory discourses surrounding women's sport during the inter-war period in Britain and reports on how these discourses impacted upon the choices that women made about their sporting apparel. Sporting women faced mixed messages and resultant pressures, such as an expectation to combine their physical activity with a feminine appearance and demeanour. Covering a range of sports, Skillen indicates that there was no particular pattern of response to this pressure. However, in one way or another, women were active in making sports clothing choices, and their increasing participation in sport during the years 1919–1939 made this a landmark period for women's sportswear.

Ann Bailey's paper looks at how the popularity of football and its players was used by the clothing industries to market their leisurewear on Britain's high streets. In his classic text, *On Human Finery*, Quentin Bell recognized the potential popularity of some sports apparel as leisurewear. However, Bell explicitly stated that this did not include football. He might then have been surprised by Bailey's research focused on the 1950s through to the mid-1970s, which reveals how footballers were modelled by clothing companies as fashion icons. The so-called 'affluent society' broadened the market for smart attire and football players took on a new and evolving role from this time on.

Geoffery Kohe draws our attention to the provocative sport-spectator practice known as 'streaking'. Streakers, much like their clothed contemporaries, are fashioned entities whose energetic efforts to disrobe and dash are imbued with historical, socio-cultural, political, and arguably aesthetic, significance. Giving regard to this range of possible meanings, Kohe contends that streakers may best be regarded not as opportunistic deviants, but rather as valid contributors to the performance spectacle. Streaking may continue to be proscribed from sports arenas, yet opportunities remain for daring experimenters to fashion new forms of sport-spectator related nudity. Accordingly, Kohe interestingly questions whether the streaking performance presents a novel and unexpected type of costume.

     DOI: 10.1179/174963012X13319136517070

In the final paper of the issue I am joined by Kevin Moore, Director of the National Football Museum, for a discussion of the symbolic significance of the shirt worn by Diego Maradona during the well-remembered quarter-final match between Argentina and England at the 1986 World Cup Finals. It was in this game that Maradona scored two of the most famous goals in the history of football, known respectively as the 'Hand of God' goal and the 'Goal of the Century'. Our paper considers the variety of meanings that the shirt may hold for different observers, but also makes a case for the shirt possessing a special aesthetic significance in its material presence as a reminder of the undisputed footballing artistry of Maradona.

Finally, I would like to thank the Editors of *Costume*, Verity Wilson and Penelope Byrde, for giving me the opportunity to work with them on this special issue. It has been my pleasure and I hope the issue proves of interest to the Journal's readership.

JOHN HUGHSON
University of Central Lancashire

*Costume*, vol. 46, no. 2, 2012

# Aquadynamics and the Athletocracy: Jennie Fletcher and the British Women's 4 × 100 metre Freestyle Relay Team at the 1912 Stockholm Olympic Games

By JEAN WILLIAMS

*This article considers the part played by aquadynamics, or a concern for the technical properties of swimming costumes, in the career of Jennie Fletcher (1890–1968) who won Britain's first individual Olympic female swimming medal (bronze) at the Stockholm Olympic Games in 1912 and contributed to the first women's team gold in the 4 × 100 metre Freestyle Relay. Her light silk one-piece racing swimsuit represented a new kind of modernity: the revealed sporting body enabled competitive principles, rather than modesty, to define the appearance of the female swimmer. The article also examines the place of the working-class competitor in our understanding of the early Games, an 'athletocracy' where performance, not background, enabled individuals to compete. The work therefore also explores the relevance of Fletcher's birthplace, Leicester, in the development of amateur and professional swimming and in the production of swmming costumes for both sport and leisure.*

KEYWORDS: *swimsuits, bathing costumes, sports dress, Olympic Games, swimming, Leicester*

*An amateur is one who has never competed for a money prize, declared wager, or staked bet; who has never taught, pursued or assisted in the practices of swimming, or any other athletic exercise, as a means of pecuniary gain; and who has not, knowingly, or without protest, taken part in any competitions with anyone who is not an amateur.*[1]

## INTRODUCTION

SINCE THE PUBLICATION of Peter Bailey's seminal work on leisure in the lives of ordinary people, it has been increasingly accepted by historians that the way people chose to spend their time, when they had the freedom to do so, is as telling as how they fulfilled their obligations in life.[2] The award of the 2012 Olympic Games to London in 2005 prompted my interest in compiling a collective biography of Britain's female competitors.[3] Most British Olympic representatives competed as amateurs, at least officially, until the mid-1980s. Athletes of all kinds therefore spent a considerable amount of their free time preparing and training for their chosen discipline.[4] Though that research is ongoing, this article focuses on one of those women: the working-class amateur swimmer Jennie Fletcher (1890–1968) and her colleagues in the British Women's 4 × 100 metre Freestyle Relay team at the 1912

DOI: 10.1179/0590887612Z.0000000006

Stockholm Olympic Games (Figure 1). The individual 100 metre Freestyle competition and the the 4 × 100 metre Freestyle Relay were the inaugural two Olympic swimming events for women, while female diving had a single class (a 10 m platform dive, in which Isabella 'Belle' White of Britain won bronze).[5] Jennie Fletcher was consequently Britain's first individual female swimming medallist (a bronze) and she contributed to the first women's team gold (in the relay). Win Hayes is therefore not quite correct in saying that Lucy Morton (1898–1980) became the first British female swimming gold medallist in 1924.[6] Few of the British public will know of Jennie Fletcher, however.

This paper is concerned with Fletcher's swimming career and so it is first of all necessary to outline the sporting context of her achievements. One commentator has suggested that, during the second half of the nineteenth century, 'Britain experienced an almost revolutionary transformation in the scale and nature of its sporting culture'.[7] The modern Olympics developed out of this, re-visioning the ancient Greek Games to suit the tastes of Anglophile French aristocrat, Pierre de Frédy, Baron de Coubertin (1863–1937). First held in Athens in 1896, the inaugural Games included British men but no women.[8] Victorian and Edwardian dress history also requires some consideration before Jennie Fletcher's life is examined in more detail:

FIGURE 1.   Isabella 'Belle' Moore, Jennie Fletcher, Annie Speirs and Irene Steer of the gold-medal winning British 4 × 100 metre Freestyle Relay team at the Olympic Games, Stockholm, 1912. The chaperone is thought to be Clara Jarvis, but a Mrs Holmes is also referred to in the official report. The cloaks that women over fourteen were required to wear by ASA rules when not swimming are evident in the bottom right of the picture

© *British Swimming, Loughborough: The British Olympic Association, London*

Lynda Nead has contextualized the 1900 Paris Olympic Games, in which women did participate, in the terms of wider developments in 'muscular looking'.[9] Nead includes the spectacle of the Olympics as part of a wider cultural paradigm-shift in which the gaze of the spectator was an active part in constructing the event: new forms of movement enabled novel perspectives in seeing and being seen.[10] The preliminary analysis of wider industry forces is therefore followed by a section on Jennie Fletcher's swimming career and the representation of her victories in 1912.

A starting point for the argument is that sporting spectacle in the Olympic Games owed much to the popularity of the great international exhibitions and the display of new technologies.[11] There is a wealth of information to support the view that all this caused considerable anxiety on behalf of those who sought to control and regulate Olympic competition.[12] The 1900 Paris and 1904 St Louis events were, for example, peripheral to great trade shows, while for Rebecca Jenkins 'the Franco-British Exhibition of 1908 became the saviour of the Olympic idea', especially the stadium built by the exhibition company.[13] There were brief proposals to include female aquatic events in London 1908: British women archers, skaters and tennis players took most of the available medals instead.[14] Meanwhile, Danish 'Lady Gymnasts' delighted some onlookers in the first London Games by wearing ankle-revealing, calf-length culottes.[15] Seeing and being seen were an inherent part of Olympic competition and the increasingly revealed athletic body an aspect of those broader processes.[16] Athletes' bodies gradually became more visible, even as the representation of those bodies in still and moving images increased with the popularity of the Olympic Games.[17]

Paradoxically, the life-stories and careers of those athletes are often invisible to the general public. This article attempts to explain how and why Jennie Fletcher came to be photographed after winning her place in Olympic history wearing a revealing racing swimsuit: in later life, she said she 'hated' the photograph (Figure 1).[18] There were clearly tensions within amateur and professional swimming at that time. The photographic evidence enables a revision of orthodoxies regarding female sporting physicality which emphasize polite rather than vigorous participation.[19] A new female Olympic aesthetic was marked in 1912 by the inclusion of a photograph of Fletcher and her colleagues in an official Games report. The racing suits, which were essentially the same as those worn in previous Games by male swimmers, were explicitly designed for competition rather than protecting the modesty of the women athletes.

This work is, then, a study in aquadynamics, defined here as the technical development of sports clothing and its embodiment. The term was first used in *Costume* in a 1990 article, 'The Englishman's Swimwear' by Richard Rutt, in which he suggested that a more scentific attitude to swimming clothing developed as late as the 1960s.[20] Rutt's dating of these innovations requires revision. The multiplicity of swimming and bathing costume design enabled the Olympic racing suits to be produced as one of many varied styles of beachwear, sea-bathing costume and athletic apparel. The promotion of a one-piece design, adapted from a gymnasium suit, pioneered by Annette Kellermann (1886–1975) is a well-known story, part of which she told herself in *How to Swim*.[21] After crossing 'three-fourths of the English channel' in 1905, Kellermann was subsequently arrested for indecency on Revere

Beach, Boston, for wearing her one-piece but was not convicted. Her case was quashed by the judge, in part, it would seem, as a late reaction to the *General Slocum* disaster on 15 June 1904. Almost one thousand passengers, mainly women and girls, drowned because they could not swim the fifty metres to the shore and safety. Kellermann made reference to the case in her defence, as well as bringing to court a man's swimsuit onto which she had sewn legs, making a suit that technically covered her from neck to ankle to meet the legal requirements of public decency at the time.[22]

We now know that the swimmers of 1912 wore silk racing suits with considerably less coverage than Kellermann's, weighing approximately two ounces.[23] As a contribution to the growing historiography of sport, dress and textile history, therefore, the 1912 Olympic competition provides an important early example of aquadynamics to contextualize contemporary debates around swimming technologies, the body and athletes' clothing.[24] This paper discusses a range of developments in sporting competition, fabric technology and dress history which converged to produce the light-weight, racing costumes at a particularly early point in women's participation in the Olympic Games (sixteen years before women's athletics were admitted the the schedule in 1928). As such, the history of Britain's Olympians requires an adjustment to include more working-class women as part of our 'athletocracy'. Sporting merit, commitment, specialist preparation and use of textile technology enabled Jennie Fletcher and her relay colleagues — Isabella 'Belle' Moore (1894–1975), Annie Speirs (1889–1926) and Irene Steer (1889–1947) — to compete at the highest level: we should therefore understand their involvement as part of a select few athletes who have represented Britain in the Olympic Games. The nostalgic view of male upper-class competitors embodying Olympic ideals is perhaps evidenced by the continuing popularity of the film *Chariots of Fire*.[25] We know comparably little about working-class Olympians, especially women, in the early part of the twentieth century. This is surprising: Lincoln Allison has argued that 'for all the insistence by public school amateurs that the only true amateur is a "gentleman", it is also true, in a clear and important sense, that working-class amateurism was a purer form than that of those for whom sport was an enhancer of curricula vitae'.[26]

Though I have yet to locate one of these swimming costumes, they are reputed to have been so gossamer-like that, in the words of the archivist at the Amateur Swimming Association (ASA), 'they would pass through a wedding ring'.[27] Aquadynamics were therefore a particular concern of swimmers between 1900 and 1912 as the technologies around the sport were becoming more advanced. This work is a small-scale study that asks what the costume worn by multiple medallist, Jennie Fletcher, meant to her as an individual and to a contemporary audience. What can this example tell us, more broadly, about dress and textile history as part of elite sports performance in the early twentieth century? While some academic and popular interest has centred on the production and consumption of the swimsuit during the inter-war period in Britain, more attention has been focused on the textile and clothing history of sport in the United States.[28] Preliminary research into the relatively neglected archives of the ASA (now known as British Swimming) at Loughborough suggested that these processes began well before the turn of the twentieth century. The many Victorian and Edwardian texts on swimming in the British Library confirmed this further. The issue has a contemporary resonance. From rather uncertain beginnings, the Olympic Games have changed dramatically to become the single biggest sports spectacle in the world today.[29] Olympic participation continues to be the most significant showcase for women athletes in the twenty-first century, though how female competitors should appear when competing remains contentious.[30] Women's boxing, for example, is to be included on the Olympic schedule for the first time in 2012, but enduringly conservative values have seen serious proposals for competitors to wear skirts while fighting.[31]

The fact that Fletcher was Leicester-born raises a further point about contingency that combines sport and textile history at a particular moment. The town not only had a thriving cross-class swimming culture when Fletcher was young but also boasted an established knitwear, hosiery and corsetry trade, as well as many boot and shoe factories. Swimming for sport and leisure consequently provided a new market for transforming underwear fabrics, techniques and styles into outerwear.[32] In addition, national links within sport and trade meant that Leicester firms clothed at least some of the British Olympic swimmers from at least 1906 until 1912 in locally sourced costumes. The contacts of Leicester-based amateur swimmer John Jarvis (1872–1933), an Olympian in 1900, 1906 and 1908, appear to have facilitated this.[33]

## THE COMMODIFICATION OF SWIMMING 1846–1912

One of the ties that bind sport and fashion is that they both look simultaneously to the future and the past. There is a broad consensus that changes in modern sport developed from folk games to 'civilized' sporting activity: a shift away from aristocratic pleasure to increasing middle-class recreation and a consequent democratization, though there remains much debate about how evolutionary or revolutionary these processes were.[34] So, though developments to commodify leisure had been strongly evident in the eighteenth century, by the end of the nineteenth, a widespread amateur ethos tried to distance itself from sport as work or as commercialized entertainment.[35] Nevertheless, as fashionable events at which to see and be seen, sport signalled the sometimes conflicting values of pleasurable indulgence, modernity, the popular, and rational use of spare time.[36]

In the second half of the nineteenth century, female sport and leisure activities included fashionable croquet, tennis and skating as well as a growing readership of newspapers, magazines, books and broad-sheets.[37] Just as croquet had shown how entrepreneurs could commodify an activity for its 'crinoline' and 'curate' participants, diversification enabled manufacturers to reinvent existing technologies for new sports markets.[38] Women began to write about, and to be written into the history of, sport in small numbers but important ways: this almost always involved a discussion of how to dress, whether one was hunting game or playing golf.[39] Contemporary publications such as *The Queen* and *The Graphic* showed women wearing new styles of clothing to ride horses, cycle, fence, sail on a yacht, play cricket or football, shoot arrows, climb the Alps and participate in ballooning, gymnastic drills, life-saving and field sports.[40] Rational dress and 'the woman question' specifically linked sport and lesiure to female emancipation.[41] With the development of the 'safety bicycle' and its mass-market production went niche consumer activities: roller-skating saw a degree of commercialization with indoor rinks (often with transitory success) catering for the middle classes and their servants, a year-round venue where men and women could mix wearing their 'best' clothes.[42]

Swimming, from the middle of the nineteenth century onwards, was referred to in contemporary accounts as an art: a means of preserving life, a vehicle for female emancipation, a risk to respectable values and a heathful means of exercise.[43] The 1846 Baths and Wash-houses Act of Parliament saw the gradual rise of the Victorian public facilities as an example of state intervention in community health, rather than leisure.[44] In contrast, Victorian associations were important, but essentially voluntaristic influences in sport. The Football Association (FA) and the Rugby Football Union (RFU), formed in 1863 and 1871 respectively, were all-male elites formed through codification: exclusionary 'laws' were intended as much for working-class men as women (who were often simply overlooked).[45] The Amateur Swimming Association (ASA), after being originally founded in 1869 as the Metropolitan Swimming Club Association, gradually came to use the word 'amateur' in its title. It had relatively little control of the sport until the mid-1880s, and, consequently, a more relaxed attitude to professionals. The title followed terms used by Amateur Athletic Association (AAA) in 1880 and the Amateur Rowing Association (ARA) in 1882.[46] Until then swimming, like cricket, tolerated amateurs and professionals side by side, though social distinction was enforced. After the mid-1880s, the influence of professional swimmers was less obvious and divides became increasingly moralized: amateurs were meant to be motivated by love and above the financial attractions that sporting excellence could bring. This could be more honoured in the breach than the observance. The most famous Victorian sportsman, cricketer W. G. Grace (1848–1915), was the most outrageous 'shamateur' of his time, and became a very wealthy man as a result.[47] As part of dictating how a person might behave within a sport, amateur laws also sought to define how a person should dress and present themselves under 'officially' sanctioned competition.[48] We might date the distinction of swimming as a sport from bathing as a pastime with the creation of the ASA, but this would be too simplistic.

Individual entrepreneurs and performers were significant. Distinguishing the sport of swimming (as a physical activity for exercise, pleasure and competition performed in rivers, newly built swimming baths and in the sea) as distinct from bathing (essentially a leisure activity, often at the sea-side) remains problematic. Though many men and women travelled to the sea to bathe, increasingly swimmers could participate in urban and rural environments.[49] The lack of clear distinction between the two extended to how to clothe the body, and in 1869 a self-appointed expert, 'Professor' Pearce, gave this insight:

Various opinions have been raised respecting the form of dress for the fair sex to use in swimming; my sister Martha introduced various fashions with great applause, but I think the best dress for swimming is a pair of loose trowsers [sic] to extend below the knees, with a loose jacket, the sleeves not to reach so far as the elbows. The jacket and trowsers are to be sewn together at the back, and tied in front with short strings, or laced, the jacket to lap over the trowsers. The dress should be of dark material, light and strong. Great heavy flannel dresses that come down to the heels are dangerous. A tall and beautiful lady had a new dress of this sort, which she showed me and advised me to recommend to my lady swimmers, but I objected to the weight and length of the same. The lady went into a neighbour's bathing machine and when bathing trod upon her dress, and was thrown forwards by the waves head foremost under the steps of the machine and before she could be extricated, she was drowned.[50]

Frederick Beckwith, amongst others, had expoited the commercial potential of swimming in Britain before the ASA was created.[51] He took the title of swimming 'Professor', as did many of his counterparts. Professor Van Glovne in New York, for example, ran a swimming 'academy' where Kate Bennett and her sisters taught middle- to upper-class women.[52] But such working-class acumen was often excluded from the amateur associations by snobbery and social convention.[53] Decidedly professional female swimmers or 'natationists' such as Beckwith's daughter Agnes and her half-sister Lizzy, combined athleticism with entertainment, coaching and teaching.[54] Agnes, for example, transferred her aquatic skills from four-mile races in the river Thames in 1875 to touring exhibitions of ornamental swimming in large glass tanks in music halls and other venues such as the Royal Aquarium, Westminster (Figure 2).[55] Being able to eat, smoke and 'sleep' underwater was an attraction at a time when fear kept most people from learning how to swim. This was, in turn, part of the expansion, diversification and nationalization of the popular music and entertainment industry that shaped sport and leisure after 1870.[56] Billed as 'The Greatest Lady Swimmer in the World', Agnes and her entourage wore considerably less than most women sea-bathers, to swim 'decoratively' in a variety of venues on a logistically challenging tour. Little surprise, then, that she married William Taylor, a theatrical agent in 1882, though she kept her well-established maiden name.[57] Agnes's show was patronised by the Prince and Princess of Wales, yet the ASA did not approve of her feats of endurance or her *costume du bain*, based on an elaborate black silk corset.

Theatre and music halls covered both high and low culture, enabling sporting performers to explore links with display, fashion and consumerism.[58] It was not unknown for the audience at Blackpool to watch a swimming pantomime or ballet and then get into the water themselves.[59] As mentioned above, there had also been some high-profile disasters that drew attention to the fact that most women and girls were not taught to swim; another example was in London in 1878 on the river Thames when a pleasure cruiser, the *Princess Alice*, sank with the loss of 640 lives, and only one woman was able to swim to safety. Between 1880 and 1914, 600 public baths were constructed in Britain.[60] Swimming was therefore varied in its forms: contemporary texts had conflicting opinions about what women should wear, though all agreed on the desirability of learning to float and being able to safely cover fifty yards to shore.[61] As Tony Mason has pointed out, national swimming events had been held in Scotland from 1892 so record-keeping and organized competition ran concurrent with for-profit activities.[62] The ASA, for example, always gave national championship races to the swimming baths that offered the highest bid as hosts partly because of its own poverty. In order to offset the cost of country-wide travel that this entailed, cheap third-class rail fares were negotiated for competitors.

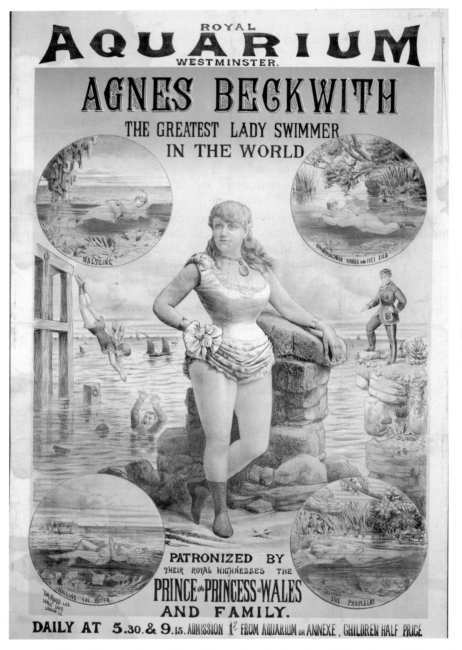

FIGURE 2.   Tom Merry, *Agnes Beckwith at Royal Aquarium, Westminster*, lithograph,
*c.* 1885. 'The greatest lady swimmer in the world 1885: Patronized by their Royal
Highnesses the Prince and Princess of Wales and family. Daily at 5.30 & 9.15.
Admission 1s/– from Aquarium or annexe, children half price'

© *The British Library Board, London (Evan.339 Royal Aquarium, Westminster)*

By 1902 the ASA had defined its own regulation swimming costumes and this remained the standard style for over twenty years, including the Olympic Games of 1924 in Paris:

At meetings where both sexes are admitted, and in all ASA Championships, competitors must wear costume in accordance with the following regulations.
a)   The colours shall be black or dark blue.
b)   Trimmings may be used ad lib.
c)   The shoulder straps shall not be less than two inches wide.
d)   It shall be buttoned at the shoulder, and the armhole cut no lower than than three inches from the armpit. Note: For ladies a shaped arm, at least three inches long shall be inserted.
e)   In the front the costume shall reach not lower than two inches below the pit of the neck. Note: For ladies the costume shall be cut straight round the neck.
f)   At the back it shall be cut straight from the top of the shoulder to top of shoulder.
g)   In the leg portion the costume shall extend to within three inches of the knee, and shall be cut in a straight line round the circumference of each leg.
h)   Drawers must be worn underneath the costume. They must be of triangular pattern, with a minumum width of 2½ inches at the fork; they must meet on each hip, and be of not less width than 3 inches on each side when fastened.
i)   On leaving the dressing room, lady competitors over 14 years of age must wear a long coat or bath gown before entering and also immediately after leaving the water.[63]

So swimming was part of a wider commercialization of sport in itself, but also an entertainment and a means of preserving life when participating in other leisure activities on, or near to, water. It was not unusual, then, that the motives for building public baths and exclusive spas in Leicester, where Jennie Fletcher was born, included a mix of civic promotion, rational welfarism and a concern for preserving the health of the urban working classes. Most large towns and small cities had at least one Victorian public bath, as much for cleansing the body as for exercising, and with strict gender segregation.[64] While the Vestry Street Baths in Leicester were the first to open in 1891, *Kelly's Directory* bragged that Cossington Street was 'one of the largest in the Kingdom'. Fridays were reserved for women. Leicester's Cossington Street Baths was a late-Victorian build, not the largest, but considered by some contemporaries the finest in the world for galas because the pool was exactly 33⅓ yards long (hence three lengths for 100 yard races) and its tiered amphitheatre accomodated 2,000 spectators.

Cross-class support for swimming was strong: Leicester County Amateur Swimming Association & Humane Society was formed with over twenty affiliated clubs in 1891 'to promote a knowledge of swimming and the resucitation [*sic*] of the apparently drowned as well as to recognise acts of bravery'.[65] The city was also enlightened in terms of having a schools' team championship from 1897 and dedicated instruction for children, at least once a week, from 1899 onwards.[66] The Leicester Ladies Swimming Club was founded and affiliated to the ASA by 1910 with Lady Faire as its President.[67] By 1912 the city also had the Leicester United Ladies Swimming Club. However, baths that might have been intended as rational hygiene facilities and places where life-saving skills could be learned, could also provide exercise and social opportunities for people of all classes.[68]

By 1912, there were at least ten public and some other baths in both the city and county of Leicester. They hosted mass-supported swimming events that Jennie

Fletcher could have seen growing up, such as the half-mile English championship in the river Soar on August Bank Holiday 1905.[69] There are two further reasons, though, that make Leicester significant, and it is worth saying a little more about both the city's textile and swimming networks, before moving on to look at Fletcher's life and career in more detail.

THE LEICESTER CONNECTION

The Leicestershire clothing industry was well placed to respond to the changes in society and culture outlined above. Leicester was an important centre of hosiery and knitwear: it was a major producer of sportswear generally, and swimwear particularly. Leicester city and Leicestershire county museums have a considerable number of surviving artefacts which include patterns, merchandising material and examples of sportswear from other local companies of national importance including Bukta, I. & R. Morley, R. & W. H. Symington and Wolsey.[70]

Nathaniel Corah had, for instance, set up as a factor in the hosiery trade, buying locally produced clothing and transporting it to the rapidly growing population of Birmingham.[71] Previously, much of the Leicester stocking trade had been home-work, done in poverty with little rationalization, and had consequently given rise to the term 'as poor as a Leicestershire stockinger'. Corah's moved in 1865 to a five-acre site near St Margaret's Church, after which the works were named. Continued success and expansion meant that it eventually employed 6,000 people in factories in the Midlands, Wales and the north of England. The first textile factory designed for integral steam-driven power, it also was also among the first to install electric lighting and power in 1883, pioneering the production of circular hose. Swimwear designs from that year demonstrated this new technology. Women's combinations and beachwear were shown side by side in the catalogue, making explicit the link between under- and outer-wear.[72] Swimsuits were just one sporting example: as well as yachting and football jerseys, golf and cycling hose, Corah's also advertised motor scarves, gloves and woollen shawls with its trademark 'Nelson' unshrinkable technology, under the St Margaret's label.[73] Corah's were internationalist in out-look: they also produced Jantzen swimwear under license from the United States manufacturer and exported goods using native-speaking agents in countries on the continental mainland.[74]

Textile technology for the mass market aside, the industry contacts of the amateur swimmer, John Jarvis, were also important for the specialized costumes that concern this article. A house-builder by trade, Jarvis had won both the 1,000 metre and 4,000 metre Freestyle swimming gold medals, in races held in the river Seine at the 1900 Olympic Games in Paris. 'Jack' Jarvis had reputation for advising both his amateur and professional rivals on technique.[75] Jarvis's wife, Ada, and his four daughters and sister also taught swimming. It is remarkable that Leicester, one of England's most inland cities, should have developed this concentration of swimming and coaching talent. Of the 356 ASA certified swimming teachers listed in the 1913 handbook, 108 were women: of these, Clara Jarvis (certificate number 73, of 80 Erskin Street), Gertrude F. Summerfield (certificate number 116, of 10 Dulverton Road) and Kathleen H. Simpson (certificate number 317, of Oaklands

Broughton Astley) were from Leicester.[76] However, it is possible to overstate the significance, as Betty Smith (the daughter of Jennie Fletcher) undoubtedly did, in later calling the city the 'cradle of modern swimming'.[77] Given the relative penury of ASA finances, John Jarvis's contacts with local swimwear manufacturers made him a vital link between athletes wishing to represent Britain in the Olympic Games and those who might clothe them in 'regulation' costumes. Specialists advertised their services in ASA yearbooks as 'Swimwear Outfitters', with the association cannily offering contests keenly entered by manufacturers who wished to become exclusive suppliers.[78]

The manufacturer A. Sills, of 260 Loughborough Road, Leicester, not only advertised his products in 1902 as 'Sole Maker by Appointment and Competition to the ASA and all the leading Swimming Clubs and Societies', he also encouraged swimmers to 'Buy Direct from the Manufacturer' (Figure 3).[79] The advertisement was accompanied by an 'Unsolicited Testimonial' from George Pragnell, the Honourable [sic] Secretary of the ASA, which included a confirmed order for 'four dozen costumes for the use of English Representatives in international matches'. Considering that the most basic women's costume of unspecified fabric started at 2s. 6d., those with cashmere trimmings increased to 3s., and a pure Milanese silk example ranged to 10s. 6d., this must have been a profitable guarantee of trade for a man whose previous attempts to sustain a business with his brothers had resulted in bankruptcy. Whereas ordinary men's bathing drawers cost 3s. 6d., the Jarvis racing slip, 'the lightest and most comfortable drawers ever produced', cost 5s. 6d. per dozen. Given these costs, it is quite likely that silk costumes were shared, repaired and recycled, accounting for some variance in appearance in the photographs that exist of men and women wearing them. However, other than being able to correspond a knitter's mark in the finish of the garment with documentary evidence for its purchase, it would be difficult to further prove the provenance of a given costume worn at any one time.

Quite how Jarvis could trade on his name in endorsing racing slips as an amateur is not clear, and we do not know if, or by how much, he profited. He was to be one of four swimmers at what became called the Intercalated Games in Athens, held in 1906, where Greece unsuccessfully attempted to become the host of the Olympics in perpetuity. Acting as Captain, Honorary Treasurer and charged with obtaining costumes 'strictly in accordance with regulations' because of his connections, Jarvis was an important leader, not just an athlete.[80] All Olympic swimmers were responsible for providing their own costumes, training costs and health needs. They were provided with one large Union flag team badge for their swimming uniform and one small version for a cloak or coat to be worn when preparing to compete. Two thirds of the £107 3s. 0d. total expenses for swimmers and officials in 1906 came from from the British Olympic Association and one third from the ASA.[81] This was spent on third-class rail and steerage boat fares, plus hotel bills.

The ASA consistently declared that it had insufficient funds to further help British entrants to Olympic Games but it had, by 1907, made links with European counterparts. On 19 July 1908, the Fédération Internationale de Natation (FINA) was formed and the ASA welcomed like-minded international amateur competition, in large part because it increased the prestige of British swimmers.[82] Oldham's

# SWIMMING COSTUMES.

Buy direct from the Manufacturer,

## A. SILLS,

### 260, Loughborough Rd., LEICESTER.

Sole Maker by appointment and competition to the Amateur Swimming Association and all the leading Swimming Clubs and Societies.

### PRICE LIST.

| A.S.A. | | Single. s. d. | ½ Doz. s. d. | 1 Doz. s. d. | Postage Paid. |
|---|---|---|---|---|---|
| | Gent's Swimming Costumes, perfect fit, can't be beaten | 1 6 | 6 6 | 12 0 | |
| | Ditto, super quality, highly recommended ... ... ... | 2 0 | 9 6 | 18 0 | |
| | Ditto, trimmed round arms and neck ... ... .. ... | 2 6 | 12 6 | 24 0 | |
| | Ditto, pure Milanese silk ... | 10 6 | — | — | |
| | Ladies' Swimming Costumes | 2 6 | 12 6 | 24 0 | |
| | Ladies' do. do. cashmere trimmings... ... | 3 0 | 16 0 | 30 0 | |

| | s. d. | s. d. | s. d. | s. d. |
|---|---|---|---|---|
| Gents' Bathing Drawers— per doz. | 3 6 | 4 6 | 5 6 | 6 6 |
| Jarvis Racing Slip ,, | 5 6 | 6 6 | — | — |

The lightest and most comfortable drawers ever produced—entirely different from the ordinary article. Worn in all the championships.

Polo Caps 3s. 6d. per set numbered.
Goal Keepers and Referees' Flags 1s. per set.

**Terms—Nett Cash with Order.**

### ☞ Unsolicited Testimonial (A.S.A.)

DEAR SIR,

"Yours are the only Costumes I have ever seen which are strictly in accordance with the A.S.A. Laws, and at the same time are so light and well cut as to satisfy our fastest swimmers. I have pleasure in enclosing you order for four dozens for the use of the English representatives in International Matches.

(Signed) GEO. PRAGNELL,

To Mr. A. SELLS. Hon. Sec. Amateur Swimming Association.

FIGURE 3. A. Sills advertisement for 'Regulation' ASA costumes including silk race-suits from the ASA yearbook of 1902. John Jarvis from Leicester made his name as a double gold medallist in the Paris Games of 1900 as a distance swimmer. Midlands underwear technologies were increasingly used in sporting outerwear. The Milanese silk suits would cost the equivalent of £45 each today

© British Swimming, Loughborough (ASA Yearbook 1902)

Henry Taylor (1885–1951) proved the wisdom of this strategy, winning three gold medals in 1908: in the 1,500 metre and 400 metres freestyle and the 4 × 200 metre freestyle relay.[83] Taylor was said to have worn a specially made costume that weighed less than an ounce which, though regulation in design, must have left little to the imagination when wet.[84] Some of the ceremonial clothing for the British team (hats, blazers and trousers or skirts) were provided by Gamages of London from 1908 onwards, but it is not clear which, if any, sporting uniforms were provided by them, too. Jennie Fletcher insisted that her costume was hand-made in Loughborough.[85]

So, although women swimmers were to appear in the Olympic Games in 1912, there were proposals that they were to do so in cumbersome swimming costumes and there was considerable debate in America, Australia, Britain and Europe about whether they should wear skirts, modesty aprons or pantaloons.[86] Was it more dangerous for the women to risk drowning or for the respectable reputation of the Olympic Games to be damaged by their inclusion? It was a dilemma that many of the swimmers, including Jennie Fletcher, were to share. The next section considers her brief swimming career and then explores how Stockholm heralded a new aesthetic for women's sport.[87] Who were the women swimmers and how did official photographs, candid snapshots and moving images of them come to be part of official reports in 1912?[88]

JENNIE FLETCHER

Fletcher swam under ASA rules, but, while her athletic career may have been helped by working-class entrepreneurialism, British amateur attitudes hindered it. She was born in 1890 to John and Emily Fletcher, who sold fruit and fish from a shop below their flat in Checkett's Road, one of the poorer parts of Leicester.[89] She was one of eleven children, of whom nine survived. According to the 1911 census, John Frederick Fletcher, a Yorkshireman, headed a house of three men and four women because the eldest two children had moved out. The census tells us that Jennie, twenty-one, worked as a cutter and machinist in a hosiery warehouse. The adolescent Fletchers also helped out at a stall on Leicester's fishmarket before going to school or work. Jennie learned to swim and won her first medal aged eleven while a pupil at Mellor Street school. Mellor Street girls' team then won the Leicester Schools Swimming Association Championship in 1903, and by 1905 Fletcher had been placed fourth in the national English 100 yards race.[90]

After her 1905 victory, Jennie Fletcher was invited to train in Southport ahead of the national championships by Alf Farrand, who was the manager of the professional swimmer, Joey Nuttall (1869–1942). (Nuttall and John Jarvis had collaborated to produce a technical innovation known as the Jarvis-Nuttall kick.) On 20 September 1906, a 2,000-strong crowd at Cossington Street Baths saw Fletcher beat Jessie Speirs to become the new English women's 100 yards freestyle champion. She was to retain her championship again from 1907 to 1909 and in 1911 and 1912. However, the gap in her dominance was indicative of a wider decline about to face British swimming. We know that Fletcher trained extensively in Vestry Baths with Leicester Ladies Swimming Club, went running in Abbey Park and combined skipping exercises with a healthy diet. She herself said that her training was limited due to a six-day working week and twelve-hour shifts.[91] In addition to fitting in her swimming commitments, she also played the piano to a reasonable standard. Nevertheless, she did train and swim extensively between 1903 and 1913. During the three-year period between 1906 and 1909, she broke her own world record eleven times; an improvement of twelve per cent.[92]

However, she nearly missed winning her bronze medal, partly because she was not swimming the crawl. In her first heat at the Stockholm Olympics on Monday

8 July 1912, Fletcher was said to have got away first but was then easily beaten by fellow British athlete Daisy Curwen. In the final, the times of the two Australians, Sarah 'Fanny' Durack and Wilhelmina Wylie, were significantly faster than Fletcher's and she fought hard against Grete Rosenborg of Germany for the bronze medal.[93] We think Jennie swam the trudgeon arms, a precursor to the crawl.[94] The ASA frowned upon the crawl as a fast but rather inelegant stroke in both its American and Australian variants. Amateur tensions as to how much a swimmer might adopt a particular stroke were, then, vital in limiting what innovation was allowed. That said, in 1908 Walter Brickett was appointed as swimming trainer to the Olympic team, reflecting the ASA concern for coaching and training, especially in view of the threat of American supremacy. Brickett appears to have been acceptable to both the ASA and the British Olympic Association (BOA) as he was to be given the title of swimming 'trainer and adviser in chief' again for 1912. Like Clara Jarvis, the chaperone and trainer for the women, he was commended in the official report of the Stockholm Games.

Jennie Fletcher was to retire in 1913 from amateur competition, having taken an appointment under the Leicester Baths Committee at Vestry Street. Given that at least three of John Jarvis's daughters and his wife had also become swimming teachers, it perhaps seemed more attractive employment than work in a factory. However, it also disqualified her from competing as an amateur. She married Henry Hyslop shortly after and moved to Ontario, Canada, to raise six children. Much of the local history material included here was provided by Betty, the youngest child, and only daughter, of this marriage. Legacy is a current obsession of the Olympic Games; on the one hand, Jennie Hyslop taught Canadian children to swim but, on the other, emigration removed her from her local and national context. She was only remembered in Leicester in the twenty-first century because of the advocacy of her surviving relatives and family friends. There is now a plaque at Cossington Baths and a star in her memory in Leicester's Walk of Fame. Her burial headstone in Teeswater, Ontario, bears the Olympic rings symbol and a comment about her swimming achievements. She was also important enough to merit an obituary in the London *Times*.[95]

As well as the photograph of 1912 that Fletcher reportedly hated, there are also images of her in a one-piece swimsuit well before this event: some with cap sleeves and with varying leg-lengths. The representation reflected conflicts that were not just about sport but also how to dress in public. Perhaps mindful of the effect of water on these fine-gauge knitted garments, the women's relay team appear with a rather intimidating chaperone, likely to be Clara Jarvis, to oversee their modesty. A new kind of modernity involving the latest technological preparation for their event is therefore offset by the clothed guardian of decency. The fact that she is so physically sturdy and 'buttoned-up' only heightens the effect. It is perhaps worth saying here that male competitors, such as Paul Günther (1882–1945) of Germany, who took part in the 1912 spring-board diving competition, wore a modesty garment or athlete's slip over, rather than under, his swimming costume. Many of the men look just as intimidated by having their photograph taken as the women. While it would go too far to interpret this as shame, there is a self-consciousness about the body language of both the men and women to suggest that this is at the limits of their comfort in being caught on camera.

The British women's relay team in Figure 1 are the first group of women Olympians to be photographed in body-revealing swimming costumes with bare heads and surprisingly dry hair. While the nipples are obvious points of punctuation in the narrative of this photograph, their bare feet are interesting, too. As a source for historians of sport, the example shares with other photographs a degree of inscrutability. Has Jennie Fletcher been dance-trained, as her stance suggests, or does this follow compositional conventions of the time in aiming the toes at ten and two o'clock? Is Belle Moore curling her toes in embarrassment or is this a spontaneous gesture? Why does Annie Speirs, of all the women, not have the Union flag on her costume? Why are the swimsuits of Irene Steer and Jennie Fletcher more opaque than those of the other two women? These are significant images showing sporting-sense rather than moral decorum dictating the dress of female athletes. They compare quite differently, for example, with the moving and still images of the demonstration of women's gymnastics which opened the Games, along with a cadre of male gymnasts, often referred to as dancers.[96] Here the men and women are dressed neck to ankle: the women in quite full skirts, even though some climb ropes in synchronized moves.

We might also ask who was left out of the picture. Of the forty-eight women who competed in Stockholm 1912 (less than 3% of the total number of the participants), none were American. The American Olympic Committee could be even more restrictive in their definitions of amateurism than the British, particularly in wanting to preserve women athletes from the gaze of male spectators. So, when Fanny Durack won the gold medal and Wilhelmina Wylie the silver for Australia, it tells us about more than their own individual appearance in Stockholm. For the 4 × 100 metres Freestyle Relay event, Australia did not send enough female swimmers and divers to form a women's relay team. The USA did not participate at all in the swimming. Jennie Fletcher, Belle Moore, Annie Speirs and Irene Steer therefore won, without the serious competition of the two nations in which the crawl had developed as the fastest stroke in freestyle swimming events. In fact, only four teams entered the 4 × 100 metre Relay and only a final competition was held: there was no need for heats. Nevertheless, women's swimming was to remain in the Olympic programme and became more international and more competitive from 1920 onwards, largely because countries increasingly came to see women athletes as a useful means of proving the superiority of their respective regimes.

Stockholm was filmed by Pathé-Frères who had commenced production in Sweden that year, ensuring world-wide distribution of the Olympic Games as newsworthy. Consequently, we have some moving-image evidence of the divers and, in addition, the still photograph of the relay team which is one of the more ubiquitous images of the Olympic Games before the First World War. There is much still to find out. Given that the female swimmers were required to wear cloaks before entering the pool and immediately after leaving it, who took this photograph? Under what circumstances were the women persuaded to pose as a group? What did they do when not competing? What did they think of the Games themselves?

CONCLUSION

From such elite racing costumes, the popular appeal of the one-piece can be better understood by cross-disciplinary analysis of dress, textile and sports history.[97] Changes in who wore what kind of swimsuit both reflected and contributed to wider processes in the British health, sport, clothing and entertainment industries. Mass production in the manufacturing sector saw technical innovations to meet new market demands, while communications technologies developed the sporting press and cinema to popularize the topical and the novel. Leicester benefited from the expanding mass market for sport and had been awarded city status in 1919 in recognition of the manufacturing role it had played in the Great War (1914–1918). By looking at the swimming clubs and the production of clothing, it is possible to see how sport and leisure increasingly linked commercial practices in which ordinary people could participate as consumers and producers. Others still, like John Jarvis, acted as important links between trades and consumers. As a hosiery factory-hand, Jennie Fletcher was as much part of the Leicester garment industry as she was part of Olympic history.

While the London Olympic Games 1908 is generally seen today to be a truly international sports tournament, it was also a chauvinistic British display of amateur superiority and a desire to win.[98] Against this, Stockholm 1912 was widely perceived to be an expensive national failure for Britain with competitors and administrators costing the BOA between £12 and £15 each to send, even when they paid for their own sports uniforms and were boarded for free in school buildings.[99] The legacy left by Fletcher and her female colleagues is that the general principle of women's participation in the Olympic Games would not be in question again (though which events were appropriate for female athletes was, and is, still contentious). Winning was always important, too: counting the total number of medals, whether won by male or female atheletes, would become another convention with which we are all familiar. Britain won nine of the available twelve women's medals in 1908, and, in 1912, women's swimming alone won Britain nine medals.[100] Given that Britain came third overall at best (depending on how the medals or points were calculated), behind the USA and Sweden, women's swimming seems to have saved the country from worse digrace. In some ways, then, the photograph of the women's 4 × 100 m Relay team gold medallists tells us as much about British sporting conservatism as it does about progressive dress history.

The evolution of swimming-costume design reflected wider changes in the Olympics and fashion industries because of the greater prominence of women athletes.[101] This aesthetic was to be revived when the Games were held in Antwerp in 1920. In the 1920s and 1930s, ideas of improved personal hygiene and the desire to keep young and beautiful were communicated through magazines, advertisements and films. Increasingly, more of the body was exposed in public and for longer periods than had been previously acceptable. Public bathing in the newly built indoor and outdoor facilities had combined sporting excellence, self-expression, self-presentation and fun. It might seem that amateur associations inhibited the interests of athletes in the short term, as in the example of the British ASA antipathy to the crawl stroke, but the prestige to be derived from Olympic competition led them to compromise their own rules in actively promoting specialized training and preparation, often provided by professional coaches. The relative financial weakness of association finances allowed 'penny entrepreneurs' and small-scale manufacturers to capitalize on niche markets, like the racing suits. At the same time, the wider commercialization of swimming enabled mass production of costumes. Further research will reveal technological innovation to exploit these diverse commercial markets, as Hannah Andrassy has indicated in her study of elasticated swimwear.[102] Apart from studying the numerous examples of swimwear in public dress collections, fashion magazines and trade catalogues can help differentiate between swimming haute couture and swimwear for the mass market. While oral histories of some British Olympic swimmers have already been collected, the Mass Observation archive at Sussex, for example, and other documents in private hands, may tell us what ordinary people thought of their swimwear or playsuits, and those of others, in the mid-twentieth century.[103]

The compelling photograph of the relay team has been often used, but the story behind it has lain dormant for almost a hundred years. We only have a few tantalizing facts about the image, and the story it tells is unfinished. Just as Britain is defining the future stars of the Olympics via new media in 2012, we are also redefining the significance of their earlier counterparts.

### REFERENCES

[1] British Olympic Council, *Olympic Games of 1908: Programme, Rules and Conditions of Competition for Swimming, Diving and Water Polo* (London: British Olympic Council, 1909), p. 4. Source: Wandsworth: British Olympic Association Library and Archive.

[2] Peter Bailey, *Leisure and Class in Victorian England* (London: Routledge, 1978).

[3] British Olympic Association, *Chasing Gold: Centenary of the British Olympic Association* (London: Getty Images, 2005).

[4] Stephanie Daniels and Anita Tedder, *A Proper Spectacle: Women Olympians 1900–1936* (Bedford: Zee Na Na Press, 2000), pp. 3–5.

[5] International Olympic Committee <http://www.olympic.org/medallists> [accessed 16 December 2011].

[6] Win Hayes, 'Lucy Morton (1898–1980)', *Oxford Dictionary of National Biography* <http://www.oxforddnb.com> [accessed 14 July 2011].

[7] Mike Huggins, *The Victorians and Sport* (Hambledon: Continuum, 2004), p. 4.

[8] Pierre de Coubertin, *Olympic Memoirs* (Lausanne: International Olympic Committee, 1997), p. 142.

[9] Lynda Nead, *The Haunted Gallery: Painting, Photography and Film c.1900* (New Haven and London: Yale University Press, 2007), pp. 34–35.

[10] Patricia Vertinsky, 'Women Sport and Exercise in the 19th Century', in *Women and Sport: Interdisciplinary Perspectives*, ed. by D. Margaret Costa and Sharon R. Guthrie (Champaign, Il: Human Kinetics 1994), pp. 70–72.

[11] For example, Aquascutum <http://www.aquascutum.com/timeline> [accessed 1 November 2011]. After trade-marking the shower-proof textile in 1853, the company of John Emery became 'Aqua-scutum' after the Latin for water-shield, following which its wrappers and coats became fashionable.

[12] British Olympic Association, Minutes of Council Meeting, 20 December 1906, Bath Club, BOA Archive, Wandsworth.

[13] Rebecca Jenkins, *The First London Olympics 1908* (London: Piaktus, 2008), p. xv.

[14] British Olympic Council, Council Meeting Minutes, 21 October 1907, 108 Victoria Street London, BOA Archive, Wandsworth, p. 6. Both the Danish and Norwegian Olympic Committees supported this request.

[15] Official Report of the Olympic Games, London 1908, BOA Archive, Wandsworth, p. 12. Also available at LA 84 Foundation <http://www.la84foundation.org> [accessed 1 November 2011].

[16] A. W. Gamage Ltd advertisement, 'The Sports House of the West', *Golf, Programme and Regulations: Olympic Games of London 1908* (London: British Olympic Council, 1908), p. 11.

[17] Patricia Campbell Warner, *When the Girls Came Out to Play* (Amherst and Boston: University of Massachusetts Press, 2006), p. 90.

[18] Sarah Staples, 'Olympian who was a Pin-up for Men and a Role Model for Women', *Leicestershire Chronicle*, 23 August 2006. Much of this article is based on interviews with Kevin McCarthy, who is writing a book on Edwardian women swimmers.

[19] *Post-Olympism?: Questioning Sport in the Twenty-First Century*, ed. by John Bale and Mette Krogh Christensen (Oxford: Berg, 2004).

[20] Richard Rutt, 'The Englishman's Swimwear', in *Costume*, 24 (1990), 69–84.

[21] Annette Kellermann, *How to Swim* (New York: George H. Doran Co., 1918), pp. 36–46.

[22] International Swimming Hall of Fame, 'From Bloomers to Bikinis: How the Sport of Swimming Changed Western Culture in the 20th Century', <http://www.ishof.org/exhibits> [accessed 14 June 2011].

[23] Philip Warren, Principal Curator of Leicestershire County Museums, kindly weighed some very fine-knit cotton and woollen costumes held in the collections from this period, and they varied between two-and-a-half to four ounces.

[24] Tara Magdalinski, *Sport, Technology and the Body: The Nature of Performance* (London: Routledge, 2008).

[25] Hugh Hudson, *Chariots of Fire* (Allied Stars/Enigma Productions, 1981); Mark Ryan *Running with Fire: The True Story of 'Chariots of Fire' Hero Harold Abrahams* (London: J. R. Books, 2011).

[26] Lincoln Allison review of *Amateurism in British Sport: It Matters Not Who Won or Lost?*, ed. by D. Porter and S. Wagg (review no. 678) <http://www.history.ac.uk/reviews> [accessed 13 October 2011].

[27] Personal communication with Wendy Coles, Amateur Swimming Association Archivist, British Swimming, Loughborough University, 14 October 2011.

[28] *Fashion V Sport* exhibition at the Victoria and Albert Museum, London, 5 August 2008–4 January 2009 <http://www.vam.ac.uk/microsites/fashion-v-sport> [accessed 2 November 2011]; *Sporting Life*, The Museum at the Fashion Institute of Technology, New York City, 25 May–5 November 2011 <http://fitnyc.edu> [accessed 2 November 2011]; 'Sally Fox Collection' Schlesinger Library Special Collections, Harvard University <http://www.radcliffe.edu/schles> [accessed 2 November 2011].

[29] Martin Polley, *The British Olympics: Britain's Olympic Heritage 1612–2012* (Swindon: Played in Britain, 2011).

[30] Allen Guttmann, *The Olympics: A History of the Modern Games* (Urbana and Chicago: University of Illinois Press, 1992; 2nd edn, 2002), preface.

[31] Paul Harris, 'London 2012: Row Over Skirts for Women Boxers Continues at ExCel', *BBC Sport 28 November 2011* <http://news.bbc.co.uk/sport1/hi/boxing> [accessed 15 December 2011].

[32] *ASA Handbook 1913 Containing a List of English Swimming Clubs; Laws of Swimming and Rules of Water Polo; Past and Present Champions and Programme for the Year*, ed. by T. M. Yeaden, ASA Secretary (Kensal Rise, NW: Hanbury, Tomsett & Co., 1913), pp. 262–63.

[33] Peter Bilsborough, 'Jarvis, John Arthur (1872–1933)', *Oxford Dictionary of National Biography* <www.oxforddnb.com/view/article/65070> [accessed 15 October 2011]. See also the International Swimming Hall of Fame entry, 'John Arthur Jarvis: Honor Swimmer 1968' <http://www.ishof.org/honorees/68/68jajarvis> [accessed 15 October 2011] giving some different interpretation of his medal tally.

[34] For a contemporary view of folk and regional games see for example, Joseph Strutt, *The Sports and Pastimes of the People of England; including the rural and domestic recreations, may games, mummeries, shows, processions, pageants and pompous spectacles from the earliest period to the present time*, ed. by William Hone (London: Thomas Tegg, 1845).

[35] Neil Tranter, *Sport, Economy and Society in Britain 1750–1914* (Cambridge: Cambridge University Press, 1998), p. 2.

[36] Peter Radford, 'Women's Foot-Races in the 18th and 19th Centuries: A Popular and Widespread Practice', in *Canadian Journal of History of Sport*, 25:1 (May 1994), 50–61; Dennis Brailsford, *A Taste for Diversions: Sport in Georgian England* (Cambridge: Lutterworth, 1999), pp. 29–30.

[37] D. M. C. Prichard, *The History of Croquet* (London: Cassell, 1981); David Drazin, *Croquet: A Bibliography Specialist Books and Pamphlets Complete to 1997* (Hampshire: St Paul's Bibliographies, 1999).

[38] Mrs Elizabeth Robins Pennell, 'Cycling', in *Ladies in the Field: Sketches of Sport*, ed. by Beatrice Violet, Baroness Greville (London: Ward and Downey Ltd, 1894), p. 264.

[39] *Ladies in the Field: Sketches of Sport*.

[40] Unknown author, 'The Ladies Archery Match in the Royal Toxophilite Society's Grounds, Regent's Park', in *The Graphic*, 9 July 1870, front page.

[41] Unknown author, 'Rational Dress for Cyclists', in *The Pall Mall Gazette* (London, Monday, 26 February 1894), p. 12.

[42] W. Arthur Deakin, *The Story of Loughborough 1888–1914* (Loughborough: Echo Press, 1979), p. 122. The Premier Roller Skating Rink lasted less than twelve months to be replaced by a café and billiards room.

[43] S. R. Powers, *Why Do Women Not Swim? Voices from Many Waters: Ladies' National Association for the Diffusion of Sanitary Knowledge* (London: Groombridge and Sons, 1859); George Forrest, *Routledge's Sixpenny Handbooks: A Handbook of Swimming and Skating* (London: Routledge, Warne and Routledge, 1860); 'Seargeant' Leahy, with Preface by Mrs Oliphant, *The Art of Swimming in the Eton Style* (London: Macmillan & Co., 1875); Captain Matthew Webb, *Swimmers' Companion* (London: R. March and Co., c. 1877); Mrs Hoggan MD, *Swimming and its Relation to the Health of Women: Read before the Women's Union Swimming Club at 36 Great Queen Street WC 21 April 1879* (Westminster: The Women's Printing Society Ltd, 1879).

[44] The Goulston Square Wash-house, one of the first built in 1846 in Whitechapel, London, was demolished but a facade preserved as part of The Women's Library, built in 2001 by London Metropolitan University <http://www.londonmet.ac.uk/about/buildings/womens-library> [accessed 17 December 2011].

[45] Lincoln Allison, *Amateurism in Sport: An Analysis and a Defence* (London: Frank Cass, 2001), pp. 165–71. Appendix 1, Chronology of Amateurism in British and Olympic Sport 1863–1995, for an overview of the formation of various sporting associations.

[46] Ian Keil and Don Wix, *In the Swim: The History of the Amateur Swimming Association from 1869 to 1994* (Leicestershire: Swimming Times Publications Ltd, 1996), pp. 35–36.

[47] David Kynaston, *W. G. 's Birthday Party* (London: Bloomsbury, 2010).

[48] Jennifer Hargreaves, *Sporting Females* (London: Routledge, 1994); *Disreputable Pleasures: Less Virtuous Victorians at Play*, ed. by Mike Huggins and J. A. Mangan (London and New York: Frank Cass, 2004); Christopher Love, *A Social History of Swimming in England, 1800–1918* (London: Routledge, 2007).

[49] Susie Parr, *The Story of Swimming* (Stockport: Dewi Lewis Publishing, 2011).

[50] Paulin Huggett Pearce, *The Warriors Swimming Book and Ladies' Guide: Including the Poem on Waterloo; Queen Victoria's Reign; Death and Funeral of the Duke of Wellington etc in two parts* (London: T. H. Roberts, 1869), pp. 15–16.

[51] Frederick Beckwith, *The Whole Art of Swimming* (London: T. Hughes, 1857).

[52] Lisa Bier, *Fighting the Current: The Rise of American Women's Swimming 1870–1926* (Jefferson, North Carolina and London: McFarland and Company, 2011), p. 15.

[53] David Day, 'From Barclay to Brickett: Coaching Practices and Coaching Lives in Nineteenth and early Twentieth Century England' (unpublished PhD thesis, De Montfort University, Leicester, 2008).

[54] David Day, '"A Modern Naiad": Nineteenth Century Female Professional Natationists', paper given at Women's History Network Women and Leisure Conference, University of Staffordshire, 8 November 2008.

[55] David Day, 'London Swimming Professors: Victorian Craftsmen and Aquatic Entrepreneurs', in *Sport in History: Special Edition Coaching Cultures*, 30:1 (2010), 32–54.

[56] Dave Russell, *Popular Music in England 1840–1914: A Social History* (Manchester and New York: Manchester University Press, 1987; revised edn, 1997), pp. 4–12.

[57] David Day, 'Professors Beckwith and Brickett: From the "Aq" to the Olympics', in Sports Coaching and the Sociological Imagination Conference, Manchester Metropolitan University, 19 March 2008, p. 3.

[58] Stephen Gundle, *Glamour: A History* (Oxford: Oxford University Press, 2008), p. 124; Sarah Kennedy, *The Swimsuit: A Fashion History from 1920s Biarritz and the Birth of the Bikini to Sportswear Styles and Catwalk Trends* (London: Carlton Books, 2007).

[59] Keith Myerscough, 'Blackpool's Triplets: Health, Pleasure and Recreation, 1875–1914' (unpublished MA Sport History and Culture Thesis, De Montfort University, Leicester, 2009), p. 45 and appendix images.

[60] Ian Gordon and Simon Inglis, *Great Lengths: The Historic Indoor Swimming Pools of Britain* (Swindon: English Heritage, 2009).

[61] A. G. Scammell, *Manual of Swimming & Diving An Illustrated Text Book* (London: Simpkin, Marshall Hamilton and Kent & Co., 1902); James H. Sterrett, *How to Swim* (New York: Spaldings Athletic Library, American Sports Publishing Co., 1903); C. M. Daniels, H. Johanson and Archibald Sinclair, *How to Swim and Save Life: Spalding's Athletic Library Vol. 11 No. 21* (London: British Sports Publishing Company Ltd, 1907).

[62] Tony Mason, *Sport in Britain* (London: Faber and Faber, 1988), p. 25.

[63] Anon., *ASA Handbook 1902 Containing List of English Swimming Clubs, Laws of Swimming and Rules of Water Polo, Past and Present Champions, Programme for the Year* (Gainsborough: J. Littlewood, 1903).

[64] Keith Myerscough, 'Nymphs, Naiads and Natation', Seventh Annual Conference of Sports History Ireland, Hunt Museum, Limerick, 10 September 2011.

[65] *Kelly's Directory of Leicestershire and Rutland 1900*, p. 528.

[66] J. A. Jarvis, *The Art of Swimming: with Notes on Polo and Aids to Life Saving* (London: Hutchinson and Co., 1902), pp. 69–72. One penny in 1901 would be equivalent to £0.35 in 2012 using the retail price index http://www.measuringworth.com [accessed 22 February 2012].

[67] *Kelly's Directory of Leicestershire and Rutland 1910*, p. 746. I could find no specific reference to other swimming clubs or to swimming teachers, though several teachers of dance, singing and so forth were listed.

[68] *Pleasure, Profit and Proselytism: British Culture and Sport at Home and Abroad 1700–1914*, ed. by J. A. Mangan (London: Frank Cass, 1988).

[69] 'Photographic pullout of Leicester images 1870–1914', in *Leicestershire Chronicle*, 23 August 2004, p. 4, captioned photograph: 'August Bank Holiday Show at the Abbey Park in 1905, when B. B. Kieron the half-mile English Championship, swimming along the river Soar'.

[70] The Symington Collection of Corsetry, Foundation and Swimwear, Leicestershire County Council Museum Service, also available at <http://museums.leics.gov.uk/collections-on-line> [accessed 1 November 2011].

[71] Corah's of Leicester 1815–1965 File, University of Leicester, Special Collections.

[72] Corah's of Leicester advertising catalogue 1912.

[73] Leicester Chamber of Commerce, *City of Leicester Year Book 1921*; Corah's of Leicester 1815–1965 File, University of Leicester, Special Collections.

[74] Jantzen labels and licence plans, Leicester County Museums Store, Barrow upon Soar, 14 August 2011.

[75] Jarvis, *The Art of Swimming*, pp. 10–15.

[76] *ASA Handbook 1913*, pp. 193–95.

[77] Betty Smith, personal communication to Steve Humphries, 15 December 2004: 'My cousin Wendy Garner and I have tried for years to interest the city in putting up plaques for all the great midland swimmers. I always think of Leicester as the "cradle of modern swimming". I guess we live too close to the Americans who make heroes of all their top athletes'.

[78] 'Swimming Outfitters', in *ASA Handbook 1913*, p. 95.

[79] A. Sills, of 260 Loughborough Road, Leicester, advertisement, *ASA Handbook 1902*, p. 262.

[80] Keil and Wix, *In the Swim*, p. 35.

[81] British Olympic Association, Council Meeting Minutes, 29 November 1906, Bath Club Dover Street, p. 5 (£107 3s. equates to £8,990 today using the retail price index http://www.measuringworth.com [accessed 22 February 2012]).

[82] The Sporting Life, *Olympic Games of London 1908: A Complete Record with Photographs of Winners of the Olympic Games Held at the Stadium Shepherd's Bush London July 13–25* (London: The Sporting Life, 1908), pp. 124–45.

[83] Peter Bilsborough, 'Taylor, Henry (1885–1951)', *Oxford Dictionary of National Biography* (Oxford University Press, 2004) <www.oxforddnb.com/view/article/65066> [accessed 15 June 2011].

[84] British Olympic Council, *Olympic Games of 1908 Programme and Conditions of Competition for Swimming Diving and Water Polo*, p. 4.

[85] Betty Smith, personal communication to Steve Humphries, 15 December 2004.

[86] International Olympic Committee File, 1910–12, International Olympic Committee Meeting Minutes 10 June 1910, International Olympic Committee Archive, Lausanne, pp. 5–6.

[87] Official Report of the Olympic Games Stockholm 1912, pp. 66–72, available at LA 84 Foundation <http://www.la84foundation.org> [accessed 1 November 2011].

[88] National Museum of Australia, Canberra, black-and-white photograph of 'Australian swimmers Fanny Durack and Mina Wylie with British swimmer Jennie Fletcher', object number 1998.0017.0010 <http://www.nma.gov.au/collections> [accessed 14 June 2011]; 'Australian swimmers Fanny Durack and Mina Wylie with British swimmer Jennie Fletcher', object number 1998.0017.0012 <http://www.nma.gov.au/collections> [accessed 14 June 2011]. OnlinefootageTV, 'The First Time: Women's Olympic Swimming Programme', object number 854 <http://www.onlinefootage.tv/video> [accessed 14 June 2011] shows eighteen seconds of the diving competition and there is other coverage of 1912 lasting collectively up to ten minutes <http://www.ishof.org> [accessed 14 June 2011].

[89] 'John Frederick Fletcher:1 & 3 & 5 Checkett's Road Belgrave Leicester', Schedule 35 Census of England and Wales 1911, The National Archives, London <www.nationalarchives.gov.uk> [accessed 14 October 2011].

[90] I am grateful to Steve Humphries of Leicester City Council for allowing access to the paperwork on this issue, including personal communication with Betty Smith, Jennie's only daughter of her six children.

[91] This is one of the often reported facts about her life taken from an interview after the 1964 Tokyo Games and just before her death, aged seventy-eight, in Canada. I have not been able to trace this interview, but the excerpt from the family material says, 'Jennie was asked to compare the athletes of the present and those of 60 years earlier. "We did not have the time or the training, we swam only after working hours and they were 12 hours and 6 days weeks"'.

[92] Kevin McCarthy, personal communication to Steve Humphries, 14 November 2004.

[93] 'Plate 36 Winners in the Fifth Olympiad Fanny Durack 100 m Free-style Ladies' (*sic*) and 'Great Britain's team in 400m Team Race for Ladies' (*sic*), Official Report of the Olympic Games Stockholm 1912, p. 851, available at LA84 Foundation <http://www.la84foundation.org> [accessed 20 June 2011]; see also National Museum of Australia, Canberra, object numbers 1998.0017.0010 and 1998.0017.0012 <http://www.nma.gov.au/collections> [accessed 14 June 2011]; 'Jennie Fletcher' <http://www.ishof.org> [accessed 14 June 2011].

[94] The images of the 1912 Official Report show her arms partly out of the water.

[95] Obituaries, 'Mrs Henry Hyslop', *The Times*, 19 January 1968, p. 10.

[96] OnlinefootageTV, 'Women's Gymnastics at the Opening Ceremony of the Vth Olympic Games' and 'Russian Dancers at the Opening Ceremony of the Vth Olympic Games', object number 854 <http://www.onlinefootage.tv/video> [accessed 14 June 2011].

[97] Charlie Lee Potter, *Sportswear in Vogue since 1910* (New York: Aberville Press, 1984).

[98] Matthew McIntire, 'National Status, the 1908 Olympic Games and the English Press', *Media History*, 15:3 (2009), 271–86.

[99] British Olympic Association, British Olympic Council Meeting Minutes, 18 July 1911, Caxton Hall, pp. 3–4; British Olympic Association, British Olympic Council Meeting Minutes, 28 November 1911, Caxton Hall, pp. 3–4. This would equate to a cost of between £927 to £1,160 per competitor and official using the retail price index http://www.measuringworth.com [accessed 22 February 2012].

[100] Using the International Olympic Committee's searchable database which counts both individual and team medals for the relay events at <http://www.olympic.org/medallists-results> [accessed 14 June 2011].

[101] Roland Renson, *La VIIème Olympiade Anvers 1920: Les Jeux Ressuscités* (Brussels: Comité Olympique et Interfédéral Belge, 1995).

[102] Hannah Andrassy, 'Spinning and Golden Thread: The Introduction of Elastic into Swimwear', *Things*, 5 (Winter 1996–97), 59–85.

[103] Private letter from George W. Hearn, Tudor House, Eltham Road, Lee, Kent, June 1924, 'Olympic Selection Letter to Gladys Carson regarding British Olympic Swimming Paris 1924', held by Gladys Carson's son David Hewitt, private collection, Hull.

JEAN WILLIAMS is a Senior Research Fellow in the International Centre for Sports History and Culture at De Montfort University, Leicester, UK. This research has been developed with the support of a De Montfort University Research Investment Fund grant for 2011–12 to look at the relationship between sport and fashion, particularly in the county of Leicestershire. A monograph on Britain's women Olympians 1900–2012 will be published by Manchester University Press in 2014.

*Costume*, vol. 46, no. 2, 2012

# 'It's possible to play the game marvellously and at the same time look pretty and be perfectly fit': Sport, Women and Fashion in Inter-war Britain

*By* FIONA SKILLEN

*This article will examine the development of women's increasing participation in sport and its impact on the subsequent emergence of sportswear for women in inter-war Britain. It will explore the public discourses which surrounded these women and their clothes in order to point up the complex nature of the problems women faced when making decisions about what to wear for sports activities.*

KEYWORDS: *tennis, hockey, golf, cricket, inter-war, sport, fitness, exercise, health*

INTRODUCTION

THE INTER-WAR YEARS in Britain (1919–1939) witnessed a boom in sporting participation amongst women.[1] A diverse range of physical activities were pursued with an unprecedented verve.[2] As one contemporary noted: 'Girls have rushed to the goal posts and wickets, and not to carry a hockey stick or a net ball [*sic*] is regarded as a sign of decadence and eccentricity'.[3] This phenomenon was accompanied by a frenzy of discussion in the British media. These discussions were divergent; while one camp praised women's newfound ability to play a variety of sports, the opposing camp made frequent protestations about the potential hazards such activities could wreak on the delicate female body, to say nothing of the immorality of allowing women to compete against each other in frequently rough sports.

Women's involvement in sports during this period, and in particular the very early inter-war years, was a complex process of negotiation. This negotiation covered every aspect of women's participation. It extended from the types of sports they engaged in to the venues where they played. It encompassed the rules by which they competed and the clothing they wore. This paper will address some of the debates that surrounded the rapid changes occurring in women's sport, focusing particularly on the clothing which women chose to, or were coerced into, wearing when taking part in specific activities during this period.

PUBLIC OPINION AND DEBATES

While the backlash which had met women's initial participation in sporting pastimes in the late nineteenth century had died down somewhat by the 1920s,

   DOI: 10.1179/0590887612Z.0000000007

there still remained an ongoing debate about the undermining potential of such activities. Concern over women's participation in vigorous, aggressive and physically demanding games underpinned the fear that this would erode the differences between the sexes. Sport had developed, as Dworkin and Messner have highlighted, to 'bolster middleclass males sagging ideology of "natural superiority"'.[4] They argue that these activities were used to enforce and perpetuate dominant and long-established discourses of masculinity. Women's entry into such an important masculine arena was seen by some to be a direct challenge to the *status quo* of male dominance. Others saw it as something even more troubling, and potentially irrevocably damaging, where participation in activities such as football would draw out masculine qualities in female competitors. After all, how could a woman who displayed the masculine qualities of competitiveness and aggression, so fundamental to successful participation in many of these sports on the pitch, not carry them over into her everyday life?[5]

This link between women, sport and masculinity was a dominant theme in many of the discussions of the period. Particular types of sport — those that were particularly physically demanding and competitive — were believed to endanger femininity. Competitiveness was viewed as an attractive quality in a man, but not in a young lady. By playing games such as football and hockey, which relied on a competitive team spirit and a certain amount of aggression, women were thought to be suppressing their naturally docile and submissive natures and instead cultivating more masculine traits. Similarly, there were real concerns over the impact that continued physical exertion would have on female bodies, especially young women's bodies.[6] Since women had first taken up sporting activities at the end of the nineteenth century the medical community had been divided about women and sport.[7] Some believed that over-exertion would affect a woman's ability to conceive or carry to term healthy children. As the headmistress of one girls' school wrote to *The Lancet* in the early 1920s:

I was a keen advocate of all forms of physical culture for girls however [...] the girls who took up what had been regarded as boys' games, hockey and even cricket, seemed to deteriorate. They seemed more selfish, more concentrated upon material things and material advantages [...] I saw that young women joining in strenuous games became possessed of hard muscles, a set jaw, flat chest and often a hard aggressive manner and an ungainly carriage. A girl's body is more elastic, more variable, and more easily changed than that of a boy. Nor should it be forgotten that the organs are more easily displaced.[8]

She goes on to highlight in various ways the potentially masculinizing effects of sport on women. In her experience, these women were less likely to marry. In fact many, as she phrased it, 'despised the opposite sex', preferring the company of other women, while those that did marry often had childless marriages which she links directly to their over-exertions on the sports field.

However, other medical experts argued that this was far from the case; if anything, based on new studies of the time, they believed that a regular fitness programme would enable women to not only produce healthier children but also help them to withstand the rigours of pregnancy, childbirth and modern life.[9] These were primary concerns of the 1920s and 1930s at a time when Britain's industrial superiority was being challenged and the threat of war in Europe was becoming an increasingly real prospect. Many of the advocates of women's sports took up these concerns and used them to legitimize the promotion of physical activities. For example, the foreword to a book written in 1922 about women's sports declares:

Who dare say that the part women have taken in our sports has made them less true or les tender? [...] Women's health, courage, beauty and (dare I say it?) temper have all most certainly gained. So much the better for merry England and the future of our race![10]

Sports participation was also promoted as a provider of vital skills which would enable modern women to deal with everyday challenges:

The strenuous and more or less artificial conditions under which modern women are living make them realize as they never realized before, the necessity of being perfectly fit physically if they are to enjoy any measure of health and consequently beauty [...] Primarily, physical exercises strengthen and develop the muscles, insuring ease and grace of movement, and making it possible to accomplish the daily round of work and pleasure without undue fatigue.[11]

While these health debates continued throughout the period, other debates focused on the ability and suitability of women to play certain sports based, at least in part, on pseudo-medical theories and social mores. Part and parcel of this debate was the issue of what was deemed to be suitable attire for sporting women. Images of them appeared regularly in newspapers and magazines throughout the inter-war years.[12] The cartoon, *What is the tennis girl to wear?*, highlights humorously the dilemma faced by many female players (Figure 1). The cartoon depicts various female tennis players wearing different items of clothing such as short skirts, long skirts and trousers. Alongside these images are the faces of three stern-looking gentlemen above which their speech bubbles state, 'How immodest!', 'How unhygienic!', 'How unbecoming!'. The cartoon explains that these are 'the three parrot cries that the woman who plays games has to endure'. It demonstrates both the attempts made by female players to find socially acceptable clothing and the types of criticism which they faced. These problems were not only associated with tennis, however, as we will see later in this article. There was a fine line between practicality and respectability, and it was this invisible, yet powerful, boundary which influenced the innovations in women's sportswear during this period.

## SPORT, FASHION AND MODERNITY

Female dress had traditionally linked women 'with frivolity, helplessness, compliance and inaction'. Thus changes to women's attire, such as higher hemlines and simpler designs, highlighted the new modern woman's attempt to break free from the restricting notions associated with the previous generation.[13] By changing the way she looked, the new 'modern' woman was making a statement about her intention to be more physically active and independent.[14] The inter-war years witnessed dramatic changes and alterations to women's fashions in general, and not least on the sports field. Trends which can be seen emerging in the Edwardian period took on a new momentum in the inter-war years, although it must be noted these changes did not flow smoothly. The causes of these changes and the factors influencing developments have been debated by several historians.[15]

FIGURE I. *'What is the tennis girl to wear?'*, cartoon from the *Daily Mirror*, 21 July 1923

The body, and in particular the female body, was a central focus of modernity. The new modern women's bodies were expected to be almost androgynous, and for some it seemed as if women were striving to look like young men; the ideal shape was thin, non-curvaceous and struck a balance between toned and muscular. Sport and exercise could be used to mould bodies into this idealized silhouette, but the way the body was dressed was as important as its natural shape. The inter-war years are an important watershed for modern fashion, as one writer explained in 1925: 'Today the normal young woman has discovered how to dress in a manner at once hygienic and convenient and attractive'.[16] In this period we see the gradual abandonment of corsets, long skirts and elaborate detail in favour of sleek lines. These new fashions were in stark contrast to those of earlier generations; they revealed more flesh and emphasized body movement. Every aspect of fashion was examined and redesigned, from shoes to hats, from coats to underwear. An important aspect of this new fashion was sportswear.

Until the turn of the twentieth century, sportswear had largely been the preserve of the middle and upper classes and their particular leisure pursuits. Even within these circles, clothing designed specifically for sport was limited and only activities which required garments to behave in a way different from the everyday, such as swimming and horse riding, had clothes developed especially for them. Other activities, for example tennis, were played in everyday clothes, shoes and even hats until the late Victorian and early Edwardian period. During the early twentieth century sports-specific clothing began to develop, but it was only during the 1920s and 1930s that these changes started to pick up pace as designers began to develop ranges of clothing specifically for the sports field and clubhouse. An important factor which assisted the spread of new designs in this period was the impact of mass production of clothing, advertising and the printing of cheap patterns which ensured that even those on moderate incomes could, if they wished, engage in the latest fashion trends.[17]

The advice pages and fashion columns of women's magazines of the period highlight how quickly this trend took hold, with sports clothing regularly featured alongside other garments. Almost without exception these pages discussed the most appropriate and fashionable clothing for both playing and watching sports. Whole outfits were often broken down, garment by garment, with the most fashionable colours and textiles described for each and, in some cases, particular retailers were recommended. The practicality and durability of items was emphasized and the ways they could be worn both on and off the course, court, beach and so forth were discussed. The quality of the materials and the craftsmanship were also highlighted. In 1930, golfing clothing is described as

built for the links [. . .] Sponsored by Dela, it is of Delatex waterproof tweed and prinsuede. The Molyneux jumper suit of jersey tweed may be seen at Selfridges, Oxford Street. It is for wearing when playing miget [sic] and other kinds of indoor golf including fairway and teeny tiny. It is also appropriate for wearing at Badminton.

Similarly, in the same year, skiwear is described as 'wind-proof, snow-proof and self-ventilating', while men's ski-suits are described as 'smart and workman-like, an alliance that is difficult of attainment, nevertheless unmistakable when achieved'.[18] To the modern consumer such detailed discussion comes across as hard-selling, but it would seem that consumers in the inter-war years needed to be reassured of the quality of their investment in times of economic uncertainty.

By the mid-1920s women's sports clothing for some sporting activities had changed dramatically, yet such changes had seemingly already become an accepted part of everyday life:

It is not many years since hockey-shirts reaching below the knees, with voluminous and ugly bloomers as a second line of defence, were regarded as a little risky, though instances when they ungovernably aroused the passions of the opposite sex were not easily discovered. Today you may find yourself, as I did recently, talking between events to the woman world's champion of something or other in athletics, clad like a boy in singlet, shorts, socks and shoes, without the smallest embarrassment on either side.[19]

New trends in sportswear marked the wearers out as 'modern', not just fashionable, holding a distinct set of values and a particular approach to life.[20] Many people regarded women's involvement in sport as fundamental to their new independence.[21] As one journalist put it: 'Much of the so-called emancipation of women has been brought about by their active participation in games which were originally looked upon as belonging to men alone'.[22] Others suggested that 'some modern women regard themselves as men in petticoats'.[23] Shorter skirts and sleeves were seen by some contemporaries to be a direct attempt by women to imitate men:

The claim of women to equality with men is understandable, but that so many of them should wish to imitate the appearance of the less beauteous sex is not so easy to understand.

Yet the whole tendency of feminine fashion in recent years has been in this direction. [. . .] the conquest of trousers has been steadily proceeding, women riders being the first to lay sacrilegious hands upon what they apparently regarded as a flaunting symbol of masculine superiority.[24]

Not only did sporting activities make women more muscular and masculine in nature, the clothing they chose to wear also ensured that they no longer looked feminine. '"It seems to me", a young modern woman confided the other day, "that athleticism for girls is becoming something of a national danger. We ought to pull up before we injure our physique and lose all our womanly charm."'[25]

Some contemporary sportswomen were clearly only too aware of this type of criticism and, keen to integrate themselves within certain sports, they were willing to forgo the most practical options in order to maintain a veneer of femininity.[26] Not all sports followed fashion to the same degree. Many, such as hockey and golf, had strict rules about the types of clothing that could be worn for playing.[27] Despite the rules concerning golfing attire, there was still room for possible changes. Interestingly, golf experienced far fewer radical changes to dominant styles during the period than many other sports. Horwood has suggested that this was due to the difficulties many women had experienced in their attempts to join clubs. She argues that they followed a relatively conservative pattern of dress so as not to disrupt the *status quo* any further. It is certainly true that women's golf clothing was amongst the most conventional of the period; colours remained muted and skirts and sleeves both stayed long until the early 1930s, at a time when in all other sports hemlines had risen some years before. That is not to say that golf remained stagnant until the 1930s; skirts did become sleeker and innovations in new styles of hats and shoes were commonplace. One lady golfer did, however, attempt to push women's golf fashion forward. At the English Ladies Golf Championships in 1933, Gloria Minoprio (1907–1958) attempted to play in trousers (Figure 2). The Ladies' Golf Union (LGU) were quick to act, noting that it 'deplored any departure from the traditional costume of the game', while making it clear that members of its organization and those wishing to participate in its competitions would not be allowed to play wearing trousers.[28]

Not all sportswomen were willing to make such sacrifices, choosing instead to adopt a more flexible approach by having two separate styles of clothing: one practical but perceived as less respectable and the other more conventional but less functional. This trend dominates particularly amongst games which were played within private grounds. For example, early hockey players playing within the confines of the school grounds, away from the public gaze, often wore shorter-than-regulation hockey tunics, shortened old school skirts or even shorts.[29] While the All-England Women's Hockey Association endorsed a standardization of tunics which would be donned for public matches, AEWHA rules stated that 'tunics shall be not less than one and not more than three inches off the ground when the player kneels'.[30] This style of tunic became popular for a number of girls' and women's sports played in schools and colleges (Figures 3 and 4).

For those who did decide to embrace changes, the debate continued between established notions of decency versus practicality. There is little doubt that these new styles were far more practical for the new athletic woman; shorter sleeves and

FIGURE 2. Woollen trousers, polo neck sweater and turban in navy blue worn by Gloria Minoprio at the 1933 English Ladies Amateur Championship. The Women Golfers' Collection
*With kind permission of the British Golf Museum, St Andrews*

skirts allowed greater freedom to stretch for a wayward ball or play out of a bunker. The abandonment of restrictive corsets and tight-fitting clothes gave women greater mobility, kept them cooler and made breathing easier. It was these practical considerations which underpinned the development of many of the new styles of sports clothing. As one female golfer explained:

The second of the two reasons for the general improvement I have indicated, lies in the matter of dress. When one thinks of the difficulties with which the first lady golfers had to contend in the past, their efforts excite our profound admiration. Their skirts used to sweep and flounce in large voluminous folds round their feet. Without the assistance of an elastic band (the famous but unfashionable 'miss higgins') which was slipped over the knees on the putting green and sometimes through the green, it would have been practically impossible to swing the club on a windy day. Was, as it were, pinched to the smallest dimensions — a compelling fashion that could not be lightly disregarded even by enthusiasts of the game, but which were scarcely suited to a comfortable swing. Nor were matters improved by wide sleeves fluttering at the shoulders. To crown everything, a large hat was usually worn, stabbed by formidable pins from every side in order to regulate its position, and in exceptionally windy weather the security of a motor veil (how dreadful they must have been!) wreathed over everything was used as an additional precaution. To our present-day ideas such conditions might well be looked upon as hopeless impediments. Not that these extremes of fashion continued for very long. They were reduced by slow degrees as time went on; but not until the last dozen years or so has ladies' dress begun to be really practical [. . .] When the skirt did begin to diminish both in length and width, it started to

FIGURE 3.    The cricket team, Royal Holloway College, London, 1923.
The tunics worn in both this image and in Figure 4 are similar in design to
those worn as AEWFHA regulation. BC/PH/6/1/1 Archives, Royal Holloway,
University of London

*www.rhul.ac.uk/archives*

FIGURE 4.    The netball team, Royal Holloway College, London, 1938.
BC/PH/6/1/3 Archives, Royal Holloway, University of London

*www.rhul.ac.uk/archives*

disappear at an alarming rate. When it rose above the knees the pendulum fortunately swung slowly in the reverse direction, until now the fashion has decided on a level which seems at the moment perfectly adapted to the playing of games with the least necessary interference.[31]

In practical terms, the clothing worn to play sport could and did have an enormous impact on the style of play and the ways in which these sports developed. In particular, the clothing worn for golf in the early part of the century directly influenced the ways in which women played:

Curiously enough in the old days, hampered as the ladies must have been, they produced swings which were far more elaborate and full than the swings we use to-day. [...] That the ladies were able to follow the instructions for carrying out this swing, restricted and encumbered as they were, is a little surprising. No wonder then that the game gained in popularity as it became less contortional [sic]. One is struck too, by the fact that although all these restrictions have been done away with, far neater and less exuberant swings have been developed, which are plainer and simpler to control.[32]

While in tennis a similar picture was emerging:

When one recalls the tennis dress of a few years ago, with long skirts and long sleeves, one wonders how women ever managed to play at all. How could any one run with skirts down to her ankles and with her waist tightly confined in corsets? I wonder about the evolution of the tennis dress during the coming years. It seems nothing could be more suitable or more practical than the costumes that are worn now, and yet there will undoubtedly be changes. Already some players have given up the wearing of stockings, which is really very sensible, as stockings are only added weight, and hamper the knee considerably in running. A little sock coming just to the top of the shoe is worn instead. Unquestionably, the short-skirted and sleeveless dress and the sensible way of dressing on the court is responsible, almost more than anything else, for the great improvement that has been seen in the standard of present-day tennis for women.[33]

The transition from the cumbersome clothing of the Edwardian period to the sleeker lines of the inter-war era was not, then, an easy transition.

## ADVICE

Women sought advice about what they should wear to play sport. They wanted to know what was practical and fashionable and also what would be socially accept- able. There were two keys places offering such advice: sports manuals and women's advice columns. By the end of the inter-war years, perhaps because of the increased availability of public facilities and the popularity of many of these activities as spec- tator sports, there was an influx of books and manuals about how to play different sports for both men and women. These books were generally written by established players and covered a range of topics from playing techniques, rules, etiquette and they certainly included clothing advice. While women's magazines and fashion features focused primarily on style with practicality coming second, the opposite was true of sports advice literature. As one tennis advice book stated:

Tennis is so active that the player, running, jumping, turning, and twisting, must have as little as possible to hamper her action. Skirts, as well as sleeves should be short. The ideal length is at the centre of the knee-cap. A skirt of this length can, in no way, hamper the player running. Skirts shorter than this [...] give no greater freedom, and are usually unattractive-looking.[34]

Advice literature also stressed the hazards that inappropriate attire posed to fellow competitors: 'For a long time women ruined their game by clothes in which they played'.[35] Not only were their skirts long, heavy and difficult to move nimbly in, but as R. C. Lyle put it: 'I have seen and played with women who wore hats, which were a danger to themselves and still greater danger to their opponents, in which there was a veritable barbed wire entanglement of hatpins'.[36] And, of course, it was not just the health of the player to be considered. As a hockey manual from the early 1920s pointed out: 'Boots or shoes with high pointed heels should never be worn. The damage they do to the ground is often irreparable'.[37] For these experts, practicality was prized over fashion; serviceability ruled over style. In these advice books, women's sports clothing was intended to 'complement and facilitate rather than hinder the exercise of athletic activity'.[38]

The level of detail, however, provided by these advice books and columns varied greatly. Some were very specific; not only were the types of clothing defined but also the colours, materials and accessories. As Helen Wills (1905–1998), an international tennis player, explained in her tennis manual:

But no matter what type of outfit worn in tennis, it is always of one color — white. White stockings and white shoes are essential accessories to the correct playing outfit. [...] color can be introduced in the sweater or jumper that one wears to and from the court and while playing, if the day is cold, solid-colored sweaters are more effective than those with an all-over pattern design. Light gay colors are more pleasing than the darker shades. Some colors on the grass court are not as good as others; for example: a green sweater about the same color as the court or a pale-blue jumper are not nearly as effective as brilliant yellow or rose colored ones. The color note may be repeated in a matching head-band, or else the white visor may be worn.[39]

Wills felt that femininity was to be emphasized at all times: 'From an artistic standpoint, the pleated skirt possesses grace and beauty in action. I think that is one of the reasons why women players are often more pleasing to watch upon the court than men. The rhythm of play and the motion of the strike is carried out by the graceful swing of the skirt'.[40] She continued later:

It is true that attractive and sensible dress for tennis increases the pleasure on all sides. It is a player's duty to think seriously about her apparel. The on-looker appreciates a trim figure on the court. The player enjoys her game more if she is suitably garbed, coolly and comfortably, so that her action is in no way impeded.[41]

Although not strictly an advice column, an article in *The Times Women's Supplement* of 1920 gives quiet approval to women wearing trousers for cricket:

But cricket cannot seriously be played in any kind of a skirt. Anyone who doubts it has only to keep wicket behind a batsman in kilts. It admits of no superfluous fringes about the lower part of the body; and even the flapping end of the strap of a leg-guard and the redundant bow on a silk scarf about the waist have brought batsmen to disaster. Cricket is incompatible with any gear less close-fitting than trousers. And why not? It is not an unknown thing for girls to play cricket in trousers in the half-privacy of school playgrounds now; and I think the ladies who lifted their skirts six inches to play lawn tennis in 1877 did a bolder thing than ladies would do who took the field on any public ground to-day in cricket flannels. Whether any woman could play in first-class cricket and hope to keep her hands 'lady-like' is another matter.[42]

However, female cricketers were banned from wearing trousers because of the fear that it would encourage people to think that they wanted to emulate their male counterparts in all aspects of the game. The Women's Cricket Association (WCA) were at pains to point out that, far from wanting to imitate men, they wanted to create a new way of playing cricket which suited women. As one WCA player explained in 1934:

The word of the year was, however, Publicity. Some players shied at the very mention of it — it was considered bad form, and so to be avoided. But pictures appeared in some papers, so obviously posed, with girls in trousers [the players of the WCA wore skirts at this time], caps, headdresses, and others with bare legs, bathing costumes, all purporting to be 'Eves at the wicket', that it became obvious, even to the most rabid on the matter, that good publicity must be found, tolerated, even assisted.[43]

Women were encouraged to think carefully about what they would wear to participate in athletic activities. They were made only too aware that their figure and clothing would be scrutinized by fellow competitors and spectators alike. An advice column about the ideal swimsuit explained: 'I pointed out to my daughter what a trim and taut and tailored mermaid the modern woman had become. Said she, "I don't know. Lots of ladies look much more bulgy in the water than when they come to dinner"'.[44] The column continues to explain that this is simply because they have not taken the time to select appropriate swimwear: 'Who wants to feel like a clean-cut Channel swimmer under water, and a string bag of assorted melons the moment you start coming on shore! I don't!'.[45] The columnist goes on to recommend a particular brand of swimwear called Sea Wave which apparently prevents such a problem so that 'the whole effect is delicious and debonair'. Not only that, but the product is so versatile that 'the panties and brassiere can be wooed away from the sea and worn with enormous satisfaction on golf links and tennis court'.[46]

## FASHION SPREADS AND ADVERTISING

Fashion spreads and advertising stressed the need for sportswomen to strike a balance between practicality, comfort and up-to-the-minute fashion. Magazines such as *Tatler* and the *Ladies' Field* emphasized the importance of being seen in the right places in the latest fashions. As well as furnishing women with advice about the latest styles, fashion editors highlighted the seasons' colours while also including vital information about the practical aspects of each item. In *Tatler*, each edition featured the latest designs for specific sports. In 1933, there were whole pages dedicated to the latest fashions for women's tennis, golf, hunting, horse riding, skiing, swimming and driving. Not only goods but whole lifestyles were being promoted, and women were encouraged to be seen in the latest fashions whether they were players or just spectators. This was especially evident in the women's 'Highway of Fashion' pages that ran in every issue of *Tatler* throughout these years. Sport was often featured in these spreads with fashion journalists, who were generally anonymous, acting as advisors and offering suggestions for the forthcoming seasons. Features often had themes, such as a May 1930 example where swimwear and general 'beachwear' were discussed: 'Really smart bathing suits are never elaborate, although the colour schemes may be of the gayest'. The next issue in June featured 'Summer Sports Wear', opening the spread with 'Fashions for the summer sports are well understood at Lillywhites', pointing up the close link with brand names. And there was valuable advice on what type of hats and gloves were both practical and fashionable for driving.[47]

Advertising in these types of publication was growing substantially across the period.[48] Again, advertisers of women's sport clothing emphasized their up-to-the-minute designs, affordability, durability and femininity. Gamages, for example, advertised their ladies' sports kit as being 'beautifully made in practical, becoming styles, lined and well finished [. . .] Windproof, Rainproof and hygienic', while Lincoln Bennett proudly advertised their 'very soft, pliable and weatherproof' sports hats with the tagline: 'Men dress to please themselves [. . .] women are not so selfish'.[49] While practicality may have been uppermost, an underlying watchword concerning women sports clothing was 'femininity'.

A feature of modern advertising is the use of celebrities or sports stars to endorse products and sports-related goods. The inter-war period witnessed several such endorsements. Some products were actually designed by the stars in the style of the outfits they wore. One case is the Suzanne Lenglen tennis dresses promoted by Selfridges (Figure 5).[50] Suzanne Lenglen (1899–1938) was a leading French tennis playing throughout the inter-war years. Her fashions, both on and off the court, were the subject of much talk in the media of the time. She came to represent the distinct break from the traditional styles often worn at Wimbledon.

CONCLUSION

The growth of women's sport during the inter-war years was problematic, and the clothes that women wore to participate in these activities were often perceived as part of the problem. The social pressures on women to conform to conservative notions of femininity, gentility and fragility, coupled with their ability to be loving and functioning wives and mothers, seemed to be threatened by sport which might alter women's physiques and undermine their feminine outlook on life. Slowly perceptions changed, partly through the pursuit of medical enquiry, and partly as the result of women challenging these opinions by actually participating in sports. By the end of the period, many more women were playing sports and access to facilities had increased.[51] The inter-war years were an important watershed in many ways for modern women's sport, and the challenge of what to wear, and the debates over what was thought to be appropriate, are very much part of the story. On women's freedom of movement, Edward Shanks wrote this in the *Saturday Review*:

Tight-laced corsets, high collars, innumerable layers of petticoats, and what not else, may have (problematically) made the female form a thing of attractive mystery, but they made the average female herself very inapt [*sic*] for the action, which she was beginning to claim the right to, of leaping on moving omnibuses. [. . .]Women felt the freedom of her limbs, and since that time she has gone on unrelentingly to a degree of comfort in dress which makes man's old reproaches against her look silly. [. . .] The truth is that woman has spent the last ten years modifying her clothing without any view to sexual allurement, but without losing sight of that specially feminine character which women's clothes have always had. She has, however unconsciously, gone on the principle of admitting light and air to her skin as much as possible. She has, incidentally, evolved a dress that much conveniences the movement of her limbs. Still more incidentally, she has evolved a form of dress that is attractive.[52]

IT is safe to predict that tennis enthusiasts all the world over will be applauding the outfits pictured on this page. They have been designed by Suzanne Lenglen and carried out by Selfridges, Oxford Street, incidentally they have been exclusively photographed for The Illustrated Sporting and Dramatic by Bassano. Suzanne Lenglen prefers a one-piece garment (naturally the shorts are separate) and is very enthusiastic about the model of which back and front views are given here. An important feature of the other is the manner in which the stole belt passes through slots. These frocks are made in a variety of fabrics and in piqué with shorts complete are 30s. The Lenglen bandeau is 4s. 6d. By the way, it must be mentioned that she has discarded stockings, her legs being cleverly treated with Elizabeth Arden's Velva Beauty Film.

# MODES
# OF THE MOMENT

By LORNA CAMERON

FIGURE 5.   The Suzanne Lenglen tennis dress promoted by Selfridges, 1933. The caption, in part, reads: 'Lenglen prefers a one-piece garment (naturally the shorts are separate) [...] Available in a variety of fabrics the outfits cost 30 shillings. The Lenglen bandeau is 4s. 6d. and the daring player has dispensed with stockings, preferring instead to use Velva Beauty Film by Elizabeth Arden!'

He seems to have thought that the problem was solved but, from a woman's point of view, there was still some way to go. Some women wanted clothing which would enhance or at the very least not encumber athletic activity. Others wanted sport-specific clothing which was fashionable and marked the wearer out as a participant in the new sporting trend and thus as a 'modern girl'. Finally, there were those who wished for suitable clothing for their sports participation which did not compromise their femininity, draw unwanted attention or leave them open to criticism. The advice manuals, advertisements and articles in the press all bear witness to the multifaceted nature of sportswear in the inter-war period.

*Acknowledgements*

I would like to take this opportunity to thank the Economic and Social Research Council for funding the original research from which this piece developed. I would also like to thank the Editors of this issue for their help, especially with regard to acquiring appropriate images to accompany the text.

REFERENCES

[1] Jennifer Hargreaves, *Sporting Females: Critical Issues in the History and Sociology of Women's Sports* (London: Routledge, 1994), ch. 6, 'The Inter-war Years: Limitations and Possibilities', pp. 112–45; Mike Huggins, 'And Now for Something for the Ladies', *Women's History Review*, 16:5 (2007), 681–700.

[2] Between 1919 and 1939 the number of clubs, schools and colleges affiliated to the All England Women's Hockey Association, for example, grew from 89 to 2,100. Scotland witnessed a similar growth from eleven affiliated clubs and schools in 1900 to 186 in 1939. For further detailed discussion on the rise of sports opportunities for women, see Fiona Skillen, 'When Women Look Their Worst: Women and Sports Participation in Interwar Scotland' (unpublished doctoral thesis, University of Glasgow, 2008).

[3] 'Women and the Sport Fetish', *The Saturday Review of Politics, Literature, Science and Art*, 26 December 1931, p. 831.

[4] Shari L. Dworkin and Michael A. Messner, Just Do What?: Sport, Bodies, Gender', in *ReVisioning Gender*, ed. by Myra Marx Ferree, Judith Lorber and Beth B. Hess (Thousand Oaks, CA: Sage, 1999), pp. 341–65.

[5] Birgitte Søland, *Becoming Modern: Young Women and the Reconstruction of Womanhood in the 1920s* (Princeton: Princeton University Press, 2000), p. 52.

[6] C. Cowdroy, letter to the *Lancet*, 14 May 1921, p. 1050.

[7] Katherine McCrone, *Sport and the Physical Emancipation of English Women, 1870–1914* (London: Routledge, 1988), p.193; and Patricia Vertinsky, *Eternally Wounded Woman* (Champaign: University of Illinois Press, 1994), pp. 1–36.

[8] C. Cowdroy, letter to the *Lancet*.

[9] For an example, see 'Games for Girls', *The Times*, 9 August 1922, p. 13.

[10] Sir A. Pease, foreword to Mrs S. Menzies, *The Woman's Book of Sports* (London, 1922).

[11] Margaret Hallam, 'Physical Exercises', *The Times Women's Supplement* (October 1920), p. 60.

[12] *Illustrated London News*, 30 June 1923, pp. 1148–49.

[13] Barbara Burman, 'Racing Bodies: Dress and Pioneer Women Aviators and Racing Drivers', *Women's History Review*, 9:2 (2000), 299–326 (p. 230).

[14] Fiona Skillen, 'Women and the Sport Fetish', *International Journal for the History of Sport*, 29:5 (2012); and Søland, *Becoming Modern*.

[15] Burman, 'Racing Bodies'; Søland, *Becoming Modern*; Catherine Horwood, 'Girls Who Arouse Dangerous Passions: Women and Bathing, 1900–1930', *Women's History Review*, 9:4 (2000), 653–73.

[16] 'The Revolution in Dress', *The Saturday Review of Politics, Literature, Science and Art*, 29 August 1925, p. 230.

[17] Fiona Hackney, 'Making Modern Women, Stitch by Stitch: Dressmaking and Women's Magazines in Britain, 1919–39', in *The Culture of Sewing: Gender, Consumption and Home Dressmaking*, ed. by Barbara Burman (Oxford: Berg, 1999), pp. 73–96.

[18] 'The Highway of Fashion', *Tatler*, 1527 (October 1930); 'The Highway of Fashion', *Tatler*, 1532 (November 1930).

[19] 'The Revolution in Dress', *The Saturday Review*, 29 August 1925, p. 230.

[20] Rebecca Arnold, *The American Look: Sportswear, Fashion and the Image of Women in 1930s and 1940s New York* (London: I. B. Tauris, 2009); Catherine Horwood, 'Dressing Like Champions: Women's Tennis Wear in Interwar England', in *The Englishness of English Dress*, ed. by Christopher Breward, Becky Conekin and Caroline Cox (Oxford: Berg, 2002).

[21] McCrone, *Emancipation*, p. 247.

[22] 'Ladies in Sport', *The Times*, 15 February 1919, p. 3.

[23] Letter to the Editor from Basil Mathews, *The Times*, 4 May 1922, p. 17.

[24] *Daily Sketch*, 24 June 1931, quoted in Horwood, 'Dressing like Champions'.

[25] 'Athleticism for Women', *Quiver* (October 1921), p. 1092.

[26] Sir H. Perry Robinson, 'Why Not Polo and Racquets?', *The Times Women's Supplement* (August 1920), p. 59; Joyce Wethered, *Golfing Memories and Methods* (London: Hutchinson, 1933), pp. 180–82.

[27] K. E. Lidderdale, *Hockey for Girls and Women* (Edinburgh: Morrison and Gibb, 1923), pp. 7–8; Wills, *Tennis*, pp. 137–38.

[28] Ladies Golf Union official statement quoted in Horwood, *Keeping Up Appearances: Fashion and Class Between the Wars* (Stroud: Sutton, 2005), p. 91.

[29] Interviewee from Cheltenham Ladies College, 'Playing Like Ladies', *Sport and the British*, BBC Radio Four, 16 February 2012.

[30] Lidderdale, *Hockey for Girls and Women*, p. 6.

[31] Wethered, *Golfing Memories*, pp. 180–82.

[32] Wethered, *Golfing Memories*, pp. 180–82.

[33] Helen Wills, *Tennis* (London: Charles Scribner, 1928), pp. 141–44.

[34] Wills, *Tennis*, p. 137.

[35] R. C. Lyle, *Hockey* (1920), p. 21.

[36] Lyle, *Hockey*, p. 21.

[37] Lidderdale, *Hockey for Girls and Women*, p. 7.

[38] Nancy Rossoff, '"Corsets and high-heeled shoes are out of place in the gymnasium": Appropriate Attire for Athletic American Women, 1880–1920', Scottish Women's History Network Autumn Conference, October 2004, Glasgow.

[39] Wills, *Tennis*, pp. 137–39.

[40] Wills, *Tennis*, pp. 141–44.

[41] Wills, *Tennis*, pp. 141–44.

[42] Robinson, 'Why Not Polo and Racquets?', p. 59.

[43] Marjory Pollard, *Cricket for Women and Girls* (London: Hutchinson, 1934), p. 23.

[44] 'Dear Christine', *Nash's Pall Mall Magazine*, 93:494 (July 1934), p. 74.

[45] 'Dear Christine', p. 74.

[46] 'Dear Christine', p. 74.

[47] *Tatler*, 1510 (May 1930); and *Tatler*, 1511 (June 1930).

[48] Cynthia I. White, *Women's Magazines, 1693–1968* (London: Michael Joseph, 1970).

[49] Gamages advertisement, *Tatler*, 1239 (March 1925); Lincoln Bennett advertisement, *Tatler*, 1239 (March 1925).

[50] 'Suzanne Lenglen Dresses', advertisement 30, *Tatler*, 115 (March 1930).

[51] See note 2 above.

[52] Edward Shanks, 'The Revolution in Dress', *The Saturday Review*, 29 August 1925, p. 231.

FIONA SKILLEN is currently a Postdoctoral Researcher in the School of Sport, Tourism and the Outdoors at the University of Central Lancashire. Her PhD, completed in the Department of Economic and Social History at the University of Glasgow, focused specifically on women's participation in sport during the inter-war period. Her research interests are particularly concerned with aspects of gender, sport, politics, social policy and changes in popular culture. She is preparing a book, *Escaping the Humdrum: Women and Sports Participation in Interwar Britain*, to be published this year by Peter Lang.

*Costume*, vol. 46, no. 2, 2012

# The Clothing and Footwear Industries and Professional Football Clubs in England, 1950–1975

By ANN BAILEY

*The paper focuses on the trade that existed between the English clothing and footwear industries and various professional football clubs in England from 1950 to 1975. It examines the sponsorship deals and advertisements that featured players wearing agreed garments and accessories during high-profile media events, and questions the importance of such occasions. The events included prestigious occasions such as the Football Association (FA) Cup Final and a growing number of international competitions. Unpicking the meanings of the business relationships that developed offers an opportunity to better understand how success on the football field offered the potential for increased trade to the clothiers in a constantly shifting marketplace.*[1]

KEYWORDS: *sport, football, sports sponsorship, English clothing industries, mid-twentieth-century Britain*

INTRODUCTION

THE TOPIC OF THIS PAPER covers two decades of great change both in the football clubs themselves and in the wider society of which they were a part. A rise in employment and increased prosperity after five years of war (1939–1945) were followed by a gradual decline as economic, social and political unrest took hold in the late 1960s.[2] Throughout the period under discussion, the football clubs struggled to modernize and accommodate new demands by the players.

There is very little information available in newspaper accounts about sponsored clothing worn by football players of this period. It was only after the discovery of the archive of EMAP, a trade publisher for the fashion industry, at the London College of Fashion that information began to emerge of the trade that existed between football clubs, clothiers and shoe manufacturers. What follows concentrates primarily on information obtained from the trade magazine *Men's Wear* (1902–2002), lodged at the EMAP archive, and to a lesser extent on in-house magazines held at the National Co-operative Archive in Manchester. *Men's Wear* incorporated *Tailor and Cutter*, *Outfitter* and *Cloth and Clothes* and was established as a trade and technical journal.

The need to restore trade after the restrictions of war is discussed in the examples that follow, but must be seen in the context of other advertisements and sponsorships. *Men's Wear* featured advertisements and articles on the stars of golf, cricket,

© The Costume Society 2012

DOI: 10.1179/0590887612Z.0000000008

rugby and motor racing as well as celebrities in the media, but these were small in number and did not form part of this enquiry. Of great importance in the post-war period was the need to increase exports and bring money back into an impoverished country. One significant example of this, researched by Rosemary Harden of the Fashion Museum in Bath, is that of Margot Fonteyn (1919–1991) when acting as an ambassadress for British fashion in the 1940s.[3] The much-respected ballerina wore and modelled clothes by various fashion designers and, when abroad, her place in the media spotlight meant she was photographed wearing these clothes, and the hope was that this stimulated trade orders for the companies. Rather than a premier dancer, this present article describes famous football teams likewise being encouraged to act as ambassadors for their country.

## FOOTBALL CLUBS AND THE CLOTHING AND FOOTWEAR INDUSTRIES IN THE 1950S

The 1950s were a time of reconstruction as Britain worked to recover from the deprivations of the Second World War; food, clothing and other goods remained in short supply. Clothes rationing ended in 1949 but it was not until 1954 that all rationing finally ceased. As the decade advanced, goods slowly became more plentiful and there was a gradual move towards full employment and an increased level of affluence for some workers.[4] Between the years 1950 to 1959, the average weekly wage rose from £6 8s. to £11 2s. 6d. At the same time standard income tax fell from 9s. 6d. in the pound to 7s 9d.[5]

Professional football clubs returning to peacetime sport attempted to re-establish themselves. Like everything else, sporting goods were scarce and rationed, and it was not unknown for clubs to ask supporters to donate clothing coupons to buy sportswear.[6] Prestigious events made do with pre-war clothes, as Men's Wear noted: 'Tracksuits worn for the first time after being stored for years were worn at Wembley last Saturday'.[7] Wembley Stadium, built in 1923 in north-west London, served as England's national football stadium and hosted major events in the sport.

The football player of the immediate post-war period was little changed from his predecessor of the late nineteenth century. The professional game in England had become established in 1885, and its players were working-class men often born locally and living within the same urban environment as that of their working-class supporters.[8] Football was a defining aspect of working-class culture, a ruling passion for working men who rarely, if ever, owned cars or televisions and whose world revolved around the communal life of work, the public house and the match.[9] Large crowds routinely turned out to watch their local teams on a Saturday afternoon. While the professional players who settled back to their trade after the game's suspension during the war were paid considerably more than a skilled workman, they still remained rooted in the local community and culture and dressed in a similar fashion to that of their contemporaries of the same class.[10]

Successful and popular players had long been the talk of the supporter, but the developments of new media meant players were now recognized by a far greater audience. Cinema newsreels, then the spread of the wireless in the 1920s and finally, in the 1950s, the expansion of television to a wider, general public, meant that people not only listened to, talked and wrote about the game, but also watched it in their own homes. Television ownership rose from three million in 1954 to eight million in 1958, and sport was significant in the promotion of television to a new audience. New financial arrangements between sporting bodies and the British Broadcasting Service (the forerunner of today's British Broadcasting Corporation, the BBC) enabled important events to be shown. From 1954, *Sportsview*, a mid-week sports omnibus, was introduced by Peter Dimmock (b. 1920), a pioneering sports broadcaster during these formative years of television.[11] The programmes combined filmed events with studio commentary, and guests included sporting personalities. The BBC television channel was joined in 1955 by a rival, the Independent Television Authority (ITV), a company that ran commercial television programmes aimed predominantly at working-class viewers. Football, as well as racing, was recognized as sporting entertainment that would appeal to a significant number of people.

One of the biggest problems for advertisers wishing to promote goods nationally after the privations of war was the lack of space in newspapers. Newsprint was rationed and daily newspapers only appeared in eight-page editions. Restrictions on newsprint finally ended in December 1956. The immediate success of commercial television in 1955 was partly due to the lack of advertising space in newspapers and declining audiences at the cinema. It was this lack of advertising opportunity as well as football's popularity as a spectator sport and the desire to expand trade that encouraged clothing companies to restart the tradition of dressing players and, in so doing, share in the publicity of the event.

Throughout the football season, professional teams competed in the long-established Football League (1888) and the Football Association (FA) Cup, first played in the 1882–1883 season. The latter knock-out competition resulted in two teams playing in front of huge crowds in the final at Wembley Stadium. In the immediate post-war years, football clubs had the largest gates for many years and advertisers, such as clothing manufacturers and retailers, were keen to use the sport's popularity to promote their products. Such promotions took into account the restrictions on dress laid down by the clubs as well as the conservative nature of most male wardrobes.

Players who were contracted to a particular club were expected to conform to that club's rulings regarding dress both on and off the pitch. Football kits (or strips) provided uniformity of dress when on the pitch and, when representing the club, smart attire was expected at all times. Club blazers, often with a club badge, shirt, tie and neatly pressed trousers, were the official uniform. Suits were the alternative to the blazer, and raincoats were also permitted, often of a wool gabardine, a material that was very popular as it was so hard-wearing. These styles of dress were common to many men, and although the etiquette surrounding dress was to slowly relax, especially in leisurewear and for holiday travel abroad (for the minority who could afford it), the suit or smart jacket and trousers remained the mainstay for most male wardrobes. The photograph in Figure 1, of working-class employees on a day trip in 1950, shows the styles of clothing worn by men, all of whom wear a tie and collar even for an informal event.

**A pictorial page souvenir of the Employees' Picnic held on 21st June to Llandudno**

FIGURE 1. Employees of the Manchester and Salford Equitable Co-operative Society Ltd, dressed for an informal outing. *Herald*, an in-house newspaper of the Co-operative Society, July 1950

Evidence of this return to business of the clothing industry and retail can be found in *Men's Wear* magazine. Late in 1949, Hellawell (Sportswear) Ltd of Leeds presented Doncaster Rovers football team with moth- and shower-proof trousers.[12] Advertised the following year as the 'flannels with a future' in the Earls Court Trade Exhibition catalogue, it claimed 'Hellawell worsted type flannels [...] were made from Catophrene treated cloth, and stain and crease-resisting'. The clothes were also directed at the 'the low-price field' and perhaps considered appropriate for football players.[13] The Third Division team were set to become top of their League table and later promoted to the Second Division. In attendance when the trousers were handed over was Mr S. Lovewell, tailoring and outfitting buyer for Doncaster Co-operative Society Ltd, in whose café the presentation took place (Figure 2). This sportswear company, trading thirty miles from a successful football club, had seized on a clearly reciprocally advantageous relationship with both the club and with the Co-operative Society (founded in 1843 and later called the Co-operative Wholesale Society — CWS) which, in the 1940s, had over six hundred stores and served a mainly working-class clientele.[14]

FIGURE 2. Members of the Doncaster Rovers team receive their Hellawell moth- and shower-proof trousers. *Men's Wear*, 3 December 1949

The following year, 1950, Arsenal won the FA Cup and the victorious players were presented with Wetherdair raincoats by Mr Norman V. Dibb, managing director of Wetherdair Ltd (founded 1923).[15] Whilst sharing in the success and subsequent publicity placed the company's name in the public eye, it is not known if there were other business agreements with Arsenal. Certainly, in 1933 there is evidence of the company presenting Everton Football Club players with raincoats. In return, a photograph of the team was used as a greeting card by the company.[16] Wetherdair produced raincoats of a superior make and of their own cloth. In 1949 they advertised their product as 'made for the few; from cloth that cannot be bettered'.[17] Suits were advertised at 13 guineas (£13 13s.), expensive when compared to a later promotion of clothing in 1952 by the M. & S. Co-operative which offered suits at £7 7s. 6d. (Figure 3). Wetherdair also traded internationally, catering for an affluent consumer.[18] At first glance it seems a strange combination, a working-class sport and an elite garment but, when advertising was still so restricted, any publicity was seemingly better than none.

Clothing companies were keen to expand their markets abroad after the isolation of war and bring much-needed money back into the country. A presentation of Stormgard raincoats to Sunderland Football Club was arranged just before the team left for Istanbul, Turkey, in 1950. Stormgard was based in Sunderland and the team members were photographed with Mr E. Ditchburn, director of the company as well as chairman of Sunderland Football Club.[19] Three years earlier, an advertisement for Stormgard at the British Industries Fair, held in Earls Court, London, revealed that the company produced a wide range of clothing including raincoats, sportswear, leather clothing, suits and motor-cycle dress.[20] The re-opening of trade to the continent of Europe was a great attraction to Stormgard and other clothing manufacturers.

Arsenal Football Club was a finalist two years later in the FA Cup, 1952, and Hope Bros Ltd (founded 1899) designed a Cup Final window display at their Regent Street branch in London.[21] 'The Arsenal colours give a splash of colour to the window, with a goal net as a background. Hope Brothers are supplying the Arsenal team with their playing outfits', proclaimed *Men's Wear*.[22] Regent Street, a

travel still out of the reach of most modest earners. The Mambo hat was styled a 'flat top', with a contrasting band and shaped like a boater but made of a felted material rather than the summer straw. An article in *Men's Wear* explained why the team had been presented with such hats: 'When the Manchester United team went to Spain last week to play Real Madrid in the final leg of the European Cup semi-final they acted as ambassadors for Britain's Mambo hat styles' (Figure 6).[32]

The appearance of the players wearing the hats made by the firm of Christy (founded 1773) was part of a bigger campaign, an ambitious drive to get more men wearing hats and thereby increase sales for the ailing hat manufacturers.[33] A year before, European men's hatters had met in Paris and agreed the Mambo and Robin Hood models were to be manufactured simultaneously in England and in mainland Europe by most of the important hat-making firms. In February of that year a caption appeared in *Men's Wear*, entitled 'Flat Top', announcing the launch of two new styles of hats, the 'Robin Hood' for sportswear and the 'Mambo', a set shape with a flat top. The flat top, based on the shape of the boater, was promoted as a new look and was 'the first real hat style change[s] in decades'.[34] It was claimed to be a style that suited most men including the young. 'Mambo' can be seen in the context of the popularity of the Mambo, a vibrant dance music and in the hit record 'Mambo Italiano' sung by Rosemary Clooney (1928–2002) in 1955.[35] The Mambo hat clearly referenced something fashionable and foreign compared to the English 'Robin Hood'.

In February 1957, the Hatters' Information Centre sponsored a presentation of new styles of men's hats at Londonderry House, Park Lane, London. A promotional leaflet included in the spring edition of *Men's Wear* revealed that the product endorsers the company had chosen were men with a high media profile. 'Six young Britons, famous in sport and entertainment, will select the particular version of the New Mambo and Robin Hood hats which they themselves like to wear.'[36]

An article in 1957 in the spring edition of *Man About Town*, a magazine founded in 1952 and directed at reasonably prosperous men, further claimed: 'The flat-tops [. . .] were due for a return to power [. . .] The boater incidentally looks excellent with a dinner jacket in the summer. Remember Maurice Chevalier?'.[37] A reference

FIGURE 6. Manchester United players wearing the Mambo hats presented to them by the Hatters' Information Centre. *Men's Wear*, 20 April 1957

to the debonair Belgian-French actor (1888–1972) added continental glamour to the Mambo hat pictured in the article.

A lengthy fashion article on men's wear in the local newspaper, the *Manchester Evening News*, was published a few days before Manchester United Football Club jetted off to take part in the European Cup semi-final, played on 11 April 1957. The article described the influences of Europe on men's fashions and a relaxing of dress codes by the older man.[38] Hats, including flat tops, were included in the fashion spread. In the context of less formal fashions, the hat was presented as part of the stylish new look for sale to men of all ages.

Using the Manchester United team as ambassadors of a much wider canvassing for hat wear enabled the British manufacturers to extend their own market place and take their trade back into mainland Europe. It also gave them the opportunity to associate themselves with the new fashion trends emanating from Europe.[39] The heightened media attention of the European Cup provided a stage for the Mambo hats to be paraded by young men en route to hoped-for success.

FASHION AND PROFESSIONAL FOOTBALL IN THE 1960S

The next decade saw tremendous changes in the English football clubs. Football players had long railed against the maximum wage and the restrictive 'retain and transfer' system. After much debate and very reluctantly, the football clubs agreed to abolish the maximum wage in 1961 and two years later, the 'retain' section of the system was ruled illegal by the High Court.[40] Players now had the freedom to negotiate their own wages and choice of club. Some of the very best players were rewarded with wages far superior to the less able, and with such wealth came a new lifestyle. A small number of the most successful players became celebrities, not just heroes to the football fan, and made headlines on the front pages of popular newspapers as well as appearing on the sports back pages. George Best (1946–2005) of Manchester United Football Club was the most recognized of the celebrity football players. Such men became part of a young, celebrity culture that symbolized, for some, the 'Swinging Sixties'.[41]

The mythology of the 'Swinging Sixties', with London as its centre, has been much argued over.[42] How significant and far-reaching were its effects is questionable but, undeniably, the city became the place where new pleasures of consumption, innovative fashions and fashionable practices originated. Boutiques, with roots in the 1950s, were managed and frequented by the young who were keen to be recognized as a part of the fashion scene, though by the end of the 1960s a considerable number of these small shops had closed down. Clothes were produced on short runs that favoured new fabrics and styles, and the bright colours and designs were directed at both male and female customers. London was the centre of these changes, although other major cities were also influential in stimulating new music and entertainment, and with it came the rise of a media-generated, city-based aristocracy, some of whom were working-class in origin. This new elite of actors, photographers, fashion models, musicians, business entrepreneurs and sportsmen all socialized together.

The vibrancy felt in London was further enhanced by the euphoria of success as England won the football World Cup in 1966. Montague Burton Ltd (founded 1900, later Burton) sponsored the off-pitch outfits of the England team and they were formally photographed wearing dark suits and white shirts.[43] They were the largest clothes chain in Great Britain and produced reasonably priced, ready-to-wear as well as individually tailored suits for men.[44] Burton had a long tradition of dressing not just footballers but other sportsmen and other countries' sports teams. There appears no clear evidence of when the practice began, but promotional photographs taken in their enormous factory at Hudson Road, Burmantofts in Leeds, showed various teams touring the factory and being measured for suits. The Australian cricket team visited the factory in 1934 and 1938, and Don Bradman, their star performer and captain, was photographed being measured for a suit on 6 May 1938.[45] Football teams were also photographed visiting the factory, including Sheffield Wednesday in March 1926.[46]

For a short time in the 1960s, one football club in particular became closely associated with the stylish city scene. That club was Chelsea, close to London's trend-setting King's Road of boutiques and restaurants.[47] Supporters included some of the most fashionable and famous in the media and one of its directors was Richard Attenborough (b. 1923), actor, producer and director. In October 1965, the same year the club won the Football League, several of the players, including Chelsea captain Terry Venables, featured in an article on style in the *Daily Express*. 'Here smartly paraded by five young men from the Chelsea set, is the New Look, elegantly worn by Mr Professional Footballer 1965 [...] They have caught the fashion fever that is sweeping the world of soccer in this country.' On the opposite page, the designer Hardy Amies (1909–2003), who styled suits for the tailoring firm Hepworth, emphasized that the young, working-class man was now able to afford to be fashionable as well as 'co-ordinated and neat'. The two articles, advertising the latest in male fashions, drew on the associations between the fashionable city, a football club situated in a fashionable neighbourhood of boutiques, and the recent, youthful success of players who themselves were fashionable. This two-page article on style exhorted the young male to buy into the described modish scene.[48]

The tradition of supplying players with clothing to wear on high-profile occasions continued, and it is possible to trace the appearance of new styles. Such styles were still governed by what the clubs deemed suitable, smart attire for their players. Leicester City players, for instance, were photographed in 1961 promoting Reliance trousers. Under the heading '1st Choice for Wembley', the advertisement claimed the football team opted to wear trousers worn by 'contemporary men' and cited their popularity. 'The Leicester City Football Club like thousands of modern men all over the country chose Reliance trousers. The team are wearing Reliance at Wembley on May 6 and for their African tour.'[49] Clubs travelling abroad out of season enabled promoters to reach markets outside of their normal trade, an important consideration for the clothing company.

It was during the 1960s when the best players were now earning high wages that they became a target for others who saw an opportunity to make money and encourage the players to invest in various business opportunities. Some of the promotions were legitimate, and players such as George Best profited from them, but other, often gullible, young men lost money in these ventures.[50] There is a noticeable growth in advertisements of individual players promoting fashionable clothing, but it was not until the 1970s that players routinely employed accountants and agents to help in making advantageous financial decisions.[51]

Advertising promotions for shirts became especially popular, and football players modelled for a variety of companies. Manufacturers of shirts and clothing retailers worked hard to secure the success of their brands in a highly competitive market. There was a great deal of enthusiasm, both from the manufacturers and the customers, for the new, such as the drip-dry, Bri-nylon shirt.[52] The styles of shirts promoted by the players varied from the formal to the decorative and were made from traditional cotton or the more modern nylon fabric. In 1960, an advertisement drew on the symbolism of the duel; two players were photographed back-to-back wearing top hats and with weapons, 'prepared to settle their differences with a pistol ball in preference to regulation issue' (Figure 7).[53] David Mackay (b. 1934) of Tottenham Hotspur was pictured advertising a shirt from Cavalcade. Ronnie Clayton (1934–2010) of England and the captain of Blackburn Rovers wore an Escorto shirt, all the clothing having been presented to the teams by fabric producers Brigray Ltd (founded 1940) and purchased from retailers Ralph Taylor Ltd. Both teams were high in the League table and Blackburn Rovers were to be finalists in the FA Cup. The image was of fashionable and successful sportsmen prepared to fight 'sportingly' and with honour.

In 1963, a full-page advertisement for Peter England 'style-setting' Bri-nylon shirts featured four men who were part of a year-long, national campaign. Danny Blanchflower (1926–1993), the Tottenham Hotspur captain and 'Footballer of the Year' in 1961, was one of the endorsers. Tottenham Hotspur had won the FA Cup in 1961 and 1962, and Blanchflower had captained his side to victory against

FIGURE 7. Advertisement for shirts presented as a duel between two opposing players Dave Mackay and Ronnie Clayton. *Men's Wear*, 27 February 1960

Atlético Madrid, in the European Cup Winners Cup in 1963. Two of the other sportsmen were motor-racing driver Innes Ireland (1930–1993) and cricketer Ted Dexter (b. 1935), both of whom had received 'Man of Style' awards in 1962 and 1963 respectively. Tellingly, the fourth man was Peter West, a BBC presenter and sports commentator, pointing up the close link between sport, the media and correct presentation. The advertisement exhorted the retailer to join in the promotion: 'National press and T.V. too! Big names in big spaces in the national press, plus a continually growing television campaign. Link up with this big promotion for Peter England and you're set for big, successful sales'.[54]

We should note that, whilst football had a mainly working-class following, racing and cricket attracted a broader audience of supporters. Racing was a year-round activity and cricket was a sport that started as football ended, although there was some overlap and overseas tours extended the season. Peter England saw the opportunity to attract considerably more retailers and consumers by featuring top sportsmen, drawn from three very popular sporting activities, who would also appear on the television throughout the year.

The advertising campaign by shirt manufacturers was not always well received. Letters to the editor of *Men's Wear* in 1968 criticized the size and distraction of advertisements at the football stadiums. One complainant wrote that 'the posters are 24 feet long and 3 feet high at the grounds end'.[55] Unfortunately for the fans, whilst these large posters were not always welcome, they could clearly be seen if the football match was being filmed.

A year after the 1966 World Cup, which made captain Bobby Moore (1941–1991) a widely known celebrity, he took part in an advertising campaign for Hornes' 'Bri-nylon Supernyl' shirts. The campaign extended to posters in the underground and on the street. In a magazine advertisement, Moore is presented as 'a star performer, young, tough and skilful', and was posed holding a book with the title 'Young Moore's Almanac'.[56] Apart from his name on the almanac there were no other references to his fame as England's captain, as the advertisers obviously expected the public to recognize him without these prompts. Moore looked stylish in a light-coloured shirt, with double cuffs, cufflinks and a dark tie. A smaller image showed Moore wearing a loose shirt and tailored trousers but, although dressed in casual clothes, he still looked well groomed. Hornes designed good-quality clothes for men who wished to look up-to-date but were not overly fashionable. It was not directed at the young teenage market but rather the young man in his twenties or older.

In 1971, a promotion in the Manchester store of Lewis featured football players supposedly visiting a Tootal shirt bar that also advertised ranges from Rael Brook, Van Heusen and Peter England (Figure 8). All these shirts were well-known brands of good quality and especially popular with young men.

Football players such as Bobby Moore and Manchester City and fellow England player Mike Summerbee (b. 1942) were tempted to invest in the shirt-making and retail industry themselves. Bobby Moore invested in a company in 1971 called 'Bobby Moore Shirts and Ties'. Mike Summerbee invested in 1968 in what was to become a successful, bespoke shirt-making business to provide an income for his

FIGURE 8.   Members of the Manchester City team in the Tootal bar of the Manchester store of Lewis during a two-week promotion by the shirt houses. *Men's Wear*, 10 June 1971

family after his retirement from football. But by the mid-1970s the shirt manufacturers and retailers were clearly struggling with the downturn in the British economy.[57] A prominent article in a 1975 issue of *Men's Wear* urged shirt-makers to buy from British mills and further restraints were demanded from the government to protect the textile industries from cheaper imports.[58] This was far from the first warning of foreign goods threatening the home market. In 1957, the Trades Union Congress received a report describing the worry felt by manufacturers as their trade was undermined by cheaper goods. There was 'a great concern in the shirt manufacturing trade about the imports of Empire produced garments [...] in the Manchester clothing industry generally, trade has been fairly steady, but there are now signs of demand easing off in many ways'.[59]

Regardless of the volatility of the clothing industry, football players and their clubs have continued to attract the attention of those keen to publicize their wares and profit from it. Whilst much has changed due to the commercialism of the sport, the same rules apply to team dress today. Smart attire is obligatory — suit, or sometimes jacket and trousers, with shirt and, preferably, a tie.

CONCLUSION

This investigation of advertisements and articles concerning football players and the clothing and footwear industries between 1950 and 1975 sheds light on an under-researched practice, one that is vitally important to understanding modern sports sponsorship. The need for the clothing companies to adapt and compete in a market that was constantly changing and under threat from outside agencies meant they looked for opportunities that would help them in their endeavours. The annual football competitions, as well as international events and foreign tours, attracted manufacturers and retailers alike who saw the potential for increased publicity and a consequent surge in sales. Key to the relationships that developed was the recognition of the media attention focused on the highest sporting achievements. Dressing the player for these elite occasions off the pitch was the ambition of those involved in the clothing and footwear industries.

## Acknowledgements

With grateful thanks to Emap Publications and the Co-operative Group for granting permission to reprint photographs sourced from their magazines.

REFERENCES

[1] Research material for this paper was sourced from Ann Bailey, 'Clothing the Professional Football Player: A Study of Fashion and Sportswear Promotions 1950–1985' (unpublished doctoral thesis, University of the Arts, London, 2008).

[2] Brian Spittles, *Britain since 1960* (Basingstoke: Macmillan, 1995).

[3] Rosemary Harden, 'Margot Fonteyn and Fashion Designers in the 1940s', *Costume*, 44 (2010), 96–105.

[4] For some young people, living at home with their parents, there was spare money to spend on leisure activities and clothing. Those aged between sixteen and twenty-six became increasingly targeted by consumer industries. For a detailed account, see Vernon Bogdanor and Robert Skidelsky, *The Age of Affluence 1951–61* (London: Macmillan, 1970).

[5] Juliet Gardiner, *From the Bomb to the Beatles* (London: Collins and Brown 1999), p. 83.

[6] Portsmouth Football Club, for example, had asked supporters to donate clothing coupons so they could buy items of dress for the players. Coupons dated 23 January 1945 were displayed at Portsmouth City Museum.

[7] *Men's Wear* (January 1946), p. 15.

[8] Professionalism in the sport enabled the introduction of a maximum wage for the player and the 'retain and transfer' system. It meant most players remained with one club unless transferred by the club owners.

[9] Richard Holt and Tony Mason, *Sport in Britain 1945–2000* (Oxford and Malden, USA: Blackwell, 2000).

[10] In 1945, players were awarded a maximum of £9 per week. Between 1951 and 1959 the maximum wage rose from £15 to £20. During the non-playing season, when wages often dropped, many players still needed to supplement their wage with other work; see Dave Russell, *Football and the English: A Social History of Association Football in England 1863–1995* (Preston: Carnegie Publishers, 1997), pp. 124–54.

[11] Gary Whannel, *Fields in Vision: Television, Sport and Cultural Transformations* (London: Routledge, 1992). Raymond Boyle and Richard Haynes, *Power Play: Sport, the Media and Popular Culture* (Essex: Pearson Education, 2000).

[12] *Men's Wear*, 3 December 1949, p. 23.

[13] Bailey, 'Clothing the Professional Football Player', pp. 88–90.

[14] Bailey, 'Clothing the Professional Football Player', pp. 88–90.

[15] *Men's Wear*, 27 May 1950, p. 23.

[16] 'Between the wars'<http://www.efchistory.co.uk> [accessed 17 January 2012].

[17] Advertisement for Wetherdair 1949, 'The Weather Coat that justifies its claim of rare distinction'. Provenance unknown.

[18] Advertisements for Wetherdair raincoats appeared in the *Sydney Morning Herald*, 19 April and 3 May 1951.

[19] *Men's Wear*, 27 May 1950, p. 25.

[20] <http://www.gracesguide.co.uk/A._Whyman> [accessed 16 January 2012].

[21] Hope Brothers was first established as a men's outfitting shop in Ludgate Hill, London, in 1874 by Thomas Peacock. Hope Brothers became a limited company in 1899.

[22] *Men's Wear*, 3 May 1952, p. 43.

[23] *Men's Wear*, 13 December 1958, p. 11.

[24] Bailey, 'Clothing the Professional Football Player', pp. 96–106.

[25] Details of Stanley Matthews' contract and subsequent ten years working for the CWS are held in the archives of the Co-operative College, Holyoake House, Hanover Street, Manchester. Numerous articles and advertisements in the various in-house magazines, including the *Herald*, 'A Star Looks On', LXI (June 1950), p. 14. For a more personal account, see Stanley Matthews, *The Way It Was: My Autobiography* (London: Headline, 2000).

[26] *Manchester Evening News*, 18 March 1950, p. 7.

[27] Umbro came to prominence in 1934 when they provided the kits for Manchester City and Portsmouth in the final of the FA Cup. The company were to provide the kits for the England squad from 1954 to 1974. For a history of the development of football kits, see Bob Bickerton, *Club Colours: An Illustrated History of Football Clubs and their Kits* (London: Hamlyn, 1998).

[28] Puma and Adidas were just two of the foreign competitors to threaten the British market, especially the boot trade.

[29] James Walvin, *The Only Game: Football in Our Times* (London: Longman, 2001), p. 203.

[30] In 1904, the French were influential in establishing the Fédération Internationale de Football Association (FIFA) and the FIFA World Cup (1930). France also played an important role in creating the Union of European Football Associations (UEFA) and the European Cup (1955).

[31] *Manchester Evening News*, 9 April, 1957.

[32] *Men's Wear*, 20 April 1957, p. 12.

[33] Penny McKnight, *Stockport Hatting* (Stockport: Stockport MBC, 2000).

[34] *Men's Wear*, 10 February 1956, p. 13.

[35] For detailed description, see Ed Morales, *The Latin Beat: The Rhythms and Roots of Latin Music from Bossa Nova to Salsa and Beyond* (Cambridge, MA: Da Capo Press, 2003). Whilst the emergence from America of 'rock and roll' in the mid-1950s was to have a major affect on popular music in England, other styles of music continued to be popular in England.

[36] The two male models featured wearing their choice of Mambo hat were Richard Lyon, a radio and television actor, and David Thomas, a champion golf professional.

[37] *Man About Town* (Spring 1957), p. 37. The magazine was launched by John Taylor, the then editor of the long-established tailoring trade weekly *Tailor & Cutter*.

[38] *Manchester Evening News*, 4 April 1957, p. 9.

[39] The Mambo hat was manufactured simultaneously in England and mainland Europe by most of the important hat-making firms.

[40] Russell, *Football and the English*, pp. 144–51.

[41] Christopher Booker, *The Neophiliacs: A Study of the Revolution in English Life in the Fifties and Sixties* (London: Collins, 1969); Dominic Sandbrook, *White Heat: A History of Britain in the Swinging Sixties* (London: Abacus, 2006).

[42] *Swinging Sixties: Fashion in London and Beyond 1955–1970*, ed. by Christopher Breward, David Gilbert and Jenny Lister (London and New York: V&A Publications, 2006).

[43] A photograph of the England team wearing Burton suits is held in the Getty Archive.

[44] In 1953, Burton stopped manufacturing cloth in response to rapidly changing fashions. Katrina Honeyman, 'Montague Burton Ltd: The Creators of Well-Dressed Men', in *Leeds City Business: Essays Marking the Incorporation of the City of Leeds*, ed. by John Chartres and Katrina Honeyman (Leeds: Leeds University Press, 1993), pp. 186–216.

[45] Photographs of these events can be found on <http://wyascatablogue.wordpress.com/tag/burtons/> [accessed 18 January 2012].

[46] West Yorkshire Archive Service (WYAS Leeds). Burton Archive WYL 1951. Photographs 118 5/4.

[47] Hunter Davies, *The Glory Game* (Edinburgh: Mainstream Sport, 1972), p. 216 for reference to Chelsea.

[48] *Daily Express*, 22 October 1965, pp. 17–18.

[49] *Men's Wear*, 6 May 1961, p. v.

[50] Bailey, 'Clothing the Professional Football Player', pp. 199–204.

[51] Bailey, 'Clothing the Professional Football Player', pp. 120–67.

[52] British Nylon Spinners invented the name Bri-Nylon and gave fashion shows at the Royal Albert Hall with designers, including Hardy Amies. ICI's Crimplene was claimed to be the fibre success story of the 1960s.

[53] *Men's Wear*, 27 February 1960, p. 42.

[54] *Men's Wear*, 9 February 1963, p. 6.

[55] *Men's Wear*, 7 November 196, pp. 9 and 12.

[56] *Sunday Times Magazine*, 4 June 1967.

[57] Bailey, 'Clothing the Professional Football Player', pp. 149 and 161.

[58] *Men's Wear*, 1 May 1975, p. 21.

[59] *Men's Wear*, 11 May 1957, p. 10.

ANN BAILEY has lectured in both further and higher education. She received her doctorate (2008) from the London College of Fashion, University of the Arts, London. She works as an independent scholar with an interest in dress associated with sport. She is currently researching ladies' golf wear from the late nineteenth century up to the present.

*Costume*, vol. 46, no. 2, 2012

# Decorative Dashes:
# Disrobing the Practice of Streaking

*By* Geoffery Z. Kohe

*As often as some athletes don their Lycra, others are almost as frequently disrobing and dashing across sports grounds. Yet, while nude performance is accepted in such cultural domains as dance and theatre, its place in sport is contested. Taking cues from scholars who write about the body, sexuality, and nudity — Barcan (2004), Carr-Gomm (2010), Kirkpatrick (2010), Martin (1991) and Shilling (2008) — this paper explores the complexities of streaking and its intertwining associations with sport and wider social, cultural and political contexts. I consider how ongoing debates about nudity and nakedness, and about clothed and unclothed bodies, create an opportunity for us to consider streaking as a valid and aesthetically valuable practice. I argue that we might move beyond streaking as an act of comical deviance, flagrant criminality or 'anti-costume', and view it as an acceptable mode of physicality with its own individual and collective meanings.*

KEYWORDS: *sport, streaking, nudity, nakedness, disrobing*

INTRODUCTION

The late Richard Martin (1947–1999), curator of the Costume Institute of the Metropolitan Museum, New York, wrote: 'As the critique of clothing becomes more and more trenchant, we are unlikely to conclude that nudism is the universal solution, but we may increasingly sympathize with those who have found that thwarting dress is more than a spiteful charge against advanced civilization'.[1] Following on from Martin's assertion, this exploratory essay proposes streaking as a costumed practice. Like those sportsmen and women dressed in a variety of specifically designed attire discussed in other articles, streaking can be viewed as a corporeal practice replete with its own definitive qualities. Streaking is 'roughly defined as running naked in public', and involves moving across an open space for self or social pleasures while partially or completely nude.[2] Ruth Barcan describes it as

a very public act, mostly performed in front of crowds. It is usually carried out by young men, sometimes in groups. It involves the exposure of the entire body, not just the penis, and that body is, literally on the run. The streaker usually aims to shock, surprise or entertain (and occasionally to self-publicize for commercial reasons). Many streakers are intoxicated, or accepting a dare.[3]

More than a mere novel and amusing form of entertainment, streaking raises questions about how naked and clothed bodies are conceptualized, the boundaries between public and private nudity and the reasons behind naked display.

          DOI: 10.1179/0590887612Z.0000000009

Joanne Entwistle and others have argued that dress and undress are loaded states inextricably tied to the human condition and the daily interactions to which it is a part.[4] Similar to the action of donning garments, the act of taking them off and deciding to dash is intentional, enmeshing streakers in corporeal politics. This paper will discuss some of streaking's meanings and, more specifically, its compatibility or otherwise with sport and sporting events. I also consider why sports arenas are such an attractive space for streaking.

THE PLEASURES OF STREAKING

For some people, nudity offers an appropriate way to counter the bodily constraints of contemporary living. Perhaps contrary to prevailing opinion, streakers can be viewed as fashioned beings. Streakers, while technically undressed, are not devoid of guise or even a certain mystique. Consider the experience of one particular group of streakers who disrobed at a session of the International Olympic Academy (situated at ancient Olympia in Greece, directly opposite the ruins of the historic sporting site).

Late one night, a group of attendees ventured out to the marble starting block at one end of the ancient stadium. They removed their clothes, or partially removed them, and tossed them carelessly on the grassy banks. Striking the appropriate starting poses they ran (or jogged) to the end of the stadium and back. They laughed (quietly), and dressed quickly, careful not to arouse the suspicions of the security guards who walked nearby. They spoke of their nude run as a celebration of the humanistic virtues of Olympic ideology; as if it was a moment worthy of immortalization.[5]

Their streaking was a nuanced act: a melange of personal pleasure, spontaneity, social motivation, humanistic ideology and collective responsibility. It took on a particular significance in the revered and respected site of sport. Similar emotions may be engendered when streaking in front of a packed stadium.

Unlike the dash in Olympia, sporting events draw large devoted crowds whose heightened arousal makes them particularly perceptive to a range of sensual experiences: the smell of hot chips, the crash of a tackle, the jeers of the crowd and, in some cases, the sight of a nude body. The crowd's reaction to the streaker is an inherent part of the action of streaking. For the streakers themselves 'there are also new bodily sensations to enjoy — the whistle of wind on the skin, the flapping of body parts — as well as the approbation of spectators, who may take vicarious as well as visual pleasure from the new social space that briefly opens up'.[6] Streaking, then, adds to the aesthetic dimensions and pleasures of sport and it may also inject a welcome respite into a game, as when a streaker disrupted the lengthy routine play of David Nalbandian and Lleyton Hewitt during the Wimbledon Men's Singles Finals in 2002; it provided some light relief from the gruelling match (Figure 1).

Sport's temporal and spatial qualities also work in streaking's favour. The central field or stage, the intervals and timeouts coupled with the short attention span of the spectators, an aura of risk and even the risqué, make sports events an opportune site for nude bodies. For some, streaking adds to the whole experience; it comprises excitement, drama, anticipation, pleasure, deviance, and unexpected bodily

FIGURE I. *Fault Lines*. A streaker dives across the net during the match between David Nalbandian and Lleyton Hewitt, Wimbledon Men's Singles Final, 2002
*© Fairfax Media*

contact. Like a range of sports, streaking is very physical; it involves bodily interactions, is defined by time and space, has certain rules and can be competitive. Like sports too, it involves strategy and tactics, is popular and has unpredictable outcomes. Yet, streaking is divisive. Some feel it desecrates the sanctity of the sports turf and distracts from the innate pleasures of watching competitive action.

## NUDITY, NAKEDNESS AND CLOTHES

Discontent over streaking and nudity is not new. Debates over the clothing and unclothing of bodies and the use of the human form as an ideological catalyst have been a prominent part of the history of civilization. In ancient Greece, for example, athletic nudity was 'the dress, one might also almost say the uniform, of the citizen who exercised in order to maintain himself in readiness for military service'.[7] Many of the arguments over nude bodies, evident also in debates over streaking, stem from historical unease about the supposed 'naturalness' of the naked human form in relation to prescribed ideas of morality. Although nudity might be conceived as natural, 'the natural state is, in fact, *unnatural*, if we accept that there have never been human societies in which the body has remained totally unclothed, decorated or adorned'.[8]

Kenneth Clark attends to this nudity-clothing dialectic in his pioneering work of 1956, *The Nude: A Study in Ideal Form*.[9] For Clark, nudity was not the same as nakedness. Rather, as an aesthetic in and of itself, nudity is a legitimate, and distinct, mode of corporeal being, culturally significant in its separation from, yet close relationship with, clothed bodies. The relationship between the two has long been fraught.[10] Yet, it is this complex relationship that makes humankind unique. Barcan surmises that, for Clark, 'nakedness is imperfect and individual; the nude is ideal and universal. Naked is nature; nudity, culture'.[11] For Carr-Gomm, 'nudity happens in art, nakedness happens in your bathroom'.[12] His distinctions are informed by the art critic, John Berger, who writes: 'To be naked is to be oneself. To be nude is to be seen by others and yet not recognized for oneself. A naked body has to be seen as an object in order to become a nude [...] The nude is condemned to never being naked. Nudity is a form of dress'.[13]

These assumptions were tested in both the USA and the UK in the 1960s and 1970s, when streaking received considerable attention from academics and the press, some of it condemnatory from conservative factions.[14] The streaking of the mid-1970s prompted several writers to try to understand the practice.[15] Murray Elkins wrote in 1974 that streaking 'is the latest attempt to erode and destroy convention, decency, and decorum and is primarily an act of [...] defiance rather than an isolated, innocuous student prank. Its precursors are long unkempt hair, dirty jeans, dirty feet, hippyism, "ups," "downs," LSD, heroin, and so-called total female liberation'.[16] Images of young people baring all at rock concerts like Woodstock and Hyde Park from 1969 onwards emboldened people to make solo dashes in public places, though group dashes also formed part of the emergent streaking culture.[17]

Across several fields, other scholars have done useful work on the body, its representations, and, specifically, the social and cultural significance of nudity and nakedness. The latter studies mostly still reside in art history, theology, sociology, feminist or cultural studies and usually in reference to criminality, deviance or anti-social behaviour. Yet, recently within sport studies close attention has been given to diverse modes of physicality and mobility.[18] A few researchers are paying closer attention to nudity and sport.[19]

Sport studies researchers have been drawn to try to understand how changing contemporary circumstances have altered the body's meanings, uses and interactions. For example, Internet avatars with virtual-world identities, new forms of media sport (such as the evolution of Ski-cross, 20/20 and Premier League Cricket, televised 'Dancing on Ice' shows, Wii-fit and fantasy sport leagues), the introduction of cyborg and biotechnologies into sport practices, and the rampant commercialization of all sorts of bodily types (such as the muscular physiques of footballer David Beckham or track athlete Jessica Ennis) as well as garments and fabrics (like swimmer Michael Phelps' controversial full body swimsuit, Anna Kournikova's revealing tennis skirts and tops, or Paralympic athlete Oscar Pistorius' synthetic appendage) have prompted new questions about sports bodies and experiences.

These new questions encompass several phenomenon, including streaking. Articles in the media demonstrate both the extensive range of nude practices and the complex and contradictory meanings ascribed to them.[20] In Australia and New Zealand — locations where streaking happens frequently — in just over six months these various items hit the headlines: 'Nude Women's Rugby Calendar Creates Stir', 'Naked Marathon Runner Gets Tasered', 'Tennis Court Streaker Hits the Wall' and 'Nude Blacks Keeping Uniform'.[21] We should also remember that it is not only nudity that causes offence but inappropriate or insufficient clothing; in this sense, the two states, clothed and unclothed, can sometimes be bracketed together.[22] Recent work in this field provides useful theoretical and evidential underpinning to help us understand streaking, which is arguably more than an act of explicit nakedness.[23]

## UNDERSTANDING AND POLICING STREAKING

While the boundary between clothed and unclothed is often blurred, it is policed to a certain extent by particular social moral codes and collective understandings about decency and appropriate civic behaviour. Streakers are an example of 'bodies who do not conform [. . .] Bodies which flout the conventions of their culture and go without their clothes are subversive of the most basic social codes and risk exclusion, scorn or ridicule'. Public intolerance of nudity, however, cannot be easily rectified by preventative measures and certainly not by a sudden shift in social or political attitudes.[24]

FIGURE 2.   Craig Simcox, *Masked Streaker*. A streaker masked in Zorro costume dashes across the pitch during the third day of the second test between New Zealand and Pakistan, January 2011
© *DominionPost (Fairfax Media)*

Streaking is only validated as a practice if it transgresses established norms and presents an affront to existing legal and social boundaries. For this to happen, the streaking must be unexpected. Those boundaries are further clouded by the partially clothed bodies of some streakers. The masked streaker in Figure 2 conceals his identity in a traditional way but leaves the intimate parts of his torso bare. He also retains his sneakers — bare feet are not usually perceived as offensive — perhaps for a quick getaway rather than for any aesthetic considerations. Likewise, the streaker in Figure 3 only wears socks and the one in Figure 4 wears just a g-string. Covering the genitalia could, arguably, be considered cheating. Yet, even the most provocative streakers (such as Mark Roberts and Lisa Lewis discussed shortly) have, at some point, donned decorative cloth in their streaking spectacles. Even when the streaker wears something, many of the same reactions are evoked — humour, shock, nervousness and surprise. As Barcan notes: 'Clothing (that necessary superfluity) is no simple beast. Its definition, function and limits are called into question all the time as part of the regular taxonomic work of all culture, such as in decisions, both implicit and explicit, about which garments count as clothes'.[25] Consider the following example:

One winter night 'discreet' notes are slipped under the bedroom doors of fifteen girls at Knox College, New Zealand's second oldest University College. It is the night before the ultimate sporting fixture, a rugby match between Knox and its historical rival Selwyn College. The next morning the girls meet secretly to prepare themselves for the task ahead. This is a mystic ritual of which the origins are uncertain. Later, at some pre-decided moment during the match, the girls dash out onto the field wearing rugby shorts, but, their torsos are entirely nude. Their 'unclothed' upper bodies have been painted in blue and white stripes and team insignia that precisely match the men's jerseys. So clever is the artistry that their streaking is not immediately obviously from afar, but still, quite apparent as they eventually near the crowd and then duck behind a nearby building to reclothe.[26]

In addition to provoking comments on gender objectification within this masculine sporting space, the streaking undertaken by this small group of Knox College women further illustrates that the practice is not necessarily a cut-and-dried matter. Rather, by creating confusing clothing boundaries and challenging conventions about nudity and its 'appropriate' public expression, the Knox women emphasize streaking's role in highlighting the contradictions over nude bodies and their ability to be constrained and defined by material conditions. 'Clothed' and 'nude' are not necessarily mutually exclusive categories.[27]

THE HISTORY AND MEANINGS OF STREAKING

Barcan and Carr-Gomm remind us that corporeal projects like streaking may appear trivial and comical but are bound up in wider social and cultural conditions. Media studies scholar, Bill Kirkpatrick, has taken on these implications and written specifically about streaking.[28] In his analysis of streaking within post-Vietnam America, drawing on John Fiske and James Carey's analysis of media events, Kirkpatrick traces the alleged origins of the practice and its exponential rise in popularity during the mid-1970s.[29] Kirkpatrick frames 1970s streaking as a specific, and exceptional, media event that was effectively a product of a distinct time and

FIGURE 3.   John Selkirk, *Sidesteps in Socks*. A streaker attempts to out-manoeuvre a security guard during a Twenty20 cricket match between New Zealand and the West Indies at Eden Park, Auckland, New Zealand, 2006

© *Fairfax Media*

social context. Amidst the chaotic landscape of progressive international social movements of the late 1960s and early 1970s, streaking grew in popularity. It reached its peak in early March 1974, when across several American states 156 incidents were reported. Streaking, and the social activism it is purported to represent, clearly aligned with related ideas about the nation's lost innocence and students' own concerns about the government control over access to higher education. Streaking was not merely a whimsical act, but a considered response to stifling contemporary conditions; it caught the popular mood.[30]

Although Kirkpatrick provides a useful contextual assessment of streaking, he does not afford the same significance to modern instances of streaking. Prolific or profound as they might seem, he feels they generally lack political or social significance.[31] However, streaking, especially as it relates to sport, is not accepted today as a harmless practice, neither does it go unchallenged. The continued negative reactions to streaking shown by members of the public, sport commentators, journalists, local authorities and those within the sports industry would attest to a practice that evidently still irks people's cultural tastes and collectively understood levels of socially acceptable behaviour.

FIGURE 4.    Anthony Phelps, *Batter Up*. Provincial cricketer, Maia Lewis, humorously
protects herself from a streaker's advance during a match in Wellington, NZ, 2002
© *DominionPost (Fairfax Media)*

Authorities in New Zealand, for example, cracked down on Hayley Jan Scheer-
hoorn who stripped (retaining only her underwear) at the rather high-brow New
Zealand Trotting Cup. Though charged with disorderly behaviour, Scheerhoorn
antics received considerable media attention, including requests to appear on
American and British television chat shows. Criticism was also levelled at Martin
Pratt who stripped (again, to his underwear) and streaked and tackled Samoan
player, Alatasi Tupou, during the popular and well-publicized International Rugby
Sevens tournament in Wellington, New Zealand. 'We take this breach of security
extremely seriously', Steve Walters, the tournament's General Manager, stated. He
continued: 'It is not acceptable to put players in that position. We regret the inci-
dent and are disappointed that one person's actions detracted from an otherwise
good first day'.[32] Pratt has subsequently been charged with assault and banned from
the stadium for two years. Similar anti-streaking sentiment has been expressed by
the English parliament and organizers for the impending 2012 London Olympic
Games who have discussed plans to fine streakers up to £20,000 for any attempts
at 'ambush marketing'. In so doing, organizers hope to protect Olympic sponsors'
commercial interests and rights.[33]
    That television producers also go to explicit lengths to avoid publicizing its
practice in sport would indicate that to disrobe and dash still means *something*, even

if that something is a practice deemed obscene and offensive. Take the BBC, for instance, which, in its official broadcasting guidelines, has a specific approach for dealing with streakers. The foremost strategy is to have an appointed person monitoring live outputs for any potential controversial or offensive material. Implemented with some discretion, the guidelines note that 'if a streaker interrupts a sporting event or other outside broadcast we should normally only show wide angles and when editorially justified'.[34]

Streaking cannot easily be written off as just a mere pastime or an obscure vocation for shameless self-promoters; strong opinions are held by those in favour of streaking, such as political and liberal rights activists, naturalists, anarchists, and students.[35] Certainly, commercial advertisers, like American online gambling site Golden Palace or telecommunications company Vodafone, stand to gain from the practice.[36]

As the quote below indicates, there are further joys to streaking:

There's something about running madly around in the altogether in front of other people that is inherently humorous. Perhaps it is the infectious glee exhibited by the often drunk runner, the absurdity of the small battle between the unclothed bravado and half-smiling authority, or the shock of seeing bare flesh in an ocean of clothing [streaking] thumbs its nose (or other appendages) at outdated public exposure laws in the true anarchic tradition of flaunting authority. It represents what we may have looked like 50,000 years ago while chasing mammoths. It livens up the cricket.[37]

For this streaker fan, body image is the issue at stake. Given the attempts by many streakers to partially cover up, crafting one's body image, or at least not showcasing certain parts of the body, is of some concern. Yet, paradoxically, once the genitalia are taken care of, it seems body image worries, particularly notions about grotesque and excess flesh, are evidently forgotten. Consider Mark Roberts, the inveterate UK streaker, who has made an occupation of streaking and who wears his nudity as proudly as any athlete might wear their own strip. By the age of forty-two, Roberts had disrupted almost every known sport and made 380 streaks.[38] For Roberts, his nudity, and in particular his almost clinical compunction to disrobe, is an important manifestation of the materiality of his own existence. That is, streaking *matters* to Roberts because it reminds him of his own physicality, a sensation he might not experience wearing clothes.

## STREAKING AND SPORT

So streaking is more complicated than merely being a diversion from sport. Rather, it is a bodily activity perhaps imbued with as many meanings as the clothed sports body. The comparison with sporting bodies here is intentional, for it is within sport, a domain that provides a captive spectator audience, that streaking may have found its last bastion.

The origins of the oldest sports and especially those founded in Ancient Greek and Roman civilizations often involved nudity and appreciation of nude athletic forms.[39] Yet, such explicit nudity is today generally perceived as an anathema to the practice and appreciation of sport. The disdain afforded streaking by some commentators, the heavy fines levied on those who disrupt sporting fixtures in this way and the general social unease all highlight the fact that, despite its historical antecedents and modern commercial value, streaking provokes condemnation within sport. There is evidently some appreciation of at least partial nudity around sport's stars: the overt sexualization of athletes like Beckham and Kournikova, and the exposure of flesh in beach volleyball. However, within the actual domain of sport — a domain, after all, for display of raw physicality and bodily performance — nudity and streaking generally remain taboo, as we have seen.

One of the most infamous and earliest sport-related streaking incidents involved Australian Michael O'Brien, who dashed across the rugby union pitch during a match between England and France at Twickenham in 1974. O'Brien was subsequently apprehended by the local police constable, Bruce Perry, who conveniently placed his hat over the offending region, a nice example of an article of clothing being deftly and imaginatively used in a way not originally intended (Figure 5). In photographer Ian Bradshaw's iconic image of the event, a bearded O'Brien appears,

FIGURE 5.   Ian Bradshaw, *Streaker Michael O'Brian Twickenham 1974*. Bradshaw's infamous image of 'Christ-like' streaker, Australian Michael O'Brien, during the Australian versus England Cricket Match, Twickenham, 1974
*Reproduced with the permission of Ian Bradshaw*

Christ-like, offering 'powerful resonances'; at least for viewers with religious persuasions.[40] O'Brien is being escorted down the sideline, restrained by three policemen while a fourth looks away. The police seem relatively jovial, yet jogging a few meters behind is a rather concerned British official, by the name of Grundy (dressed fairly formally even for 1974), coming to the rescue with his outspread raincoat, while thousands of spectators look on. Bradshaw captured many images of the event, several of which more provocatively display the genitalia. However, the photographer selected this particular image for the initial debut in the *Sunday Mirror*. O'Brien's antics were not particularly novel. Rather, O'Brien's streaking, though controversial, was part of a larger wave of incendiary streaking incidents. Despite its fame via Bradshaw's photograph, O'Brien's particular 1976 streak did not really shift perceptions about nudity on the pitch. Even now there is no widespread acceptance of the practice, nor is there a change in attitude by those who control sport.

Also, despite plenty of anecdotal evidence about the practice of streaking and its participants, ascertaining a demographic picture of streakers remains difficult. While popular in mainstream sports such as rugby union, cricket and football, streaking has also taken place in tennis, snooker, wrestling and curling. Moreover, although Kirkpatrick discussed the types of people and groups who engaged in the practice during the 1960s and 1970s, no recent comprehensive analysis exists that might help us better understand who is streaking now and why. A cursory summation of the evidence indicates that streakers are predominantly still young, white males (roughly between their late teens to early thirties). Yet, we cannot say definitely that streakers are a homogenous group. In his forties, Mark Roberts, for instance, shows little intention of halting his behaviour. There is also the case of the Knox College women who challenge streaking as a male preserve. Spaces devoted to celebrating the efforts of female streakers and the 'urban nudism' movement have opened up. Relatively recent is the emergence of streaking (luǒ bēn) in China, which challenges the extreme sensitivities of the ruling Communist regime and conservative population.[41] What is not in doubt is that sport has become the stronghold of streaking culture in a number of countries.

Consumer practices which render bodies, and especially unclothed bodies, commercially valuable, have made sporting sites ideal spaces for streaking. Sport itself is already a practice that inculcates physical pleasure. Spectators and participants in these spaces play roles in maintaining a 'sporting gaze': modes of viewing that privilege titillating displays of flesh. Thus, even before streakers begin, the pitch is already a sensually charged place.[42] Today, streaking, once a sporadic, deviant and most unpredictable action, has become so caught up with modern media sports culture that moments of nudity are effectively constrained and sometimes managed by the sporting establishment itself or by commercial enterprise. Now, when streaking does occur, any voyeuristic, aesthetic or vicarious pleasures television audiences may derive from the experience are quickly denied by savvy media companies who avert cameras away from the action. For spectators who do get to see streaking, the experience is no longer purely about nudity. A few companies, such as Golden Palace, have now taken a considerable risk to pay individuals to wear their corporate logos and streak during major sports events. These logos are generally painted on the largest bodily surface: the non-offending regions of the back and torso, for example.

There are also new challenges to the practice. During a 1996 one-day international cricket match in Australia, for instance, organizers introduced a very heavy $5,000 fine for pitch invasion. 'Potential streakers', Carr-Gomm notes, 'who previously only had a public indecency fine of $150 to fear, now had to think carefully before taking the plunge — and very few have done since'.[43] Streaking's prevalence within sport has arguably promoted the necessity for better controls, akin to those brought into force to combat football hooliganism, surely a greater threat to disorder than streaking. For some, however, the allure of streaking and ultimately its benefits have proved too great to pass up. In New Zealand, for example, streakers have continued to disrupt the cricket and rugby sevens, among other sports.[44] One of the most outstanding streakers has been former sex worker, model and compulsive streaker, Lisa Lewis, who has disrobed at a number of national sports events and has subsequently used her notoriety to earn financial endorsements, employment opportunities and social acclaim.

Yet, as liberalizing as Lewis potentially is, she exercises constraint over her corporeal politics (Figure 6). In many of her antics, Lewis chooses to be scantily clad rather than fully nude; titillation and desire for the unseen flesh perhaps come into the equation here. Lewis has, nonetheless, been a key advocate in the political battle to decriminalize streaking.[45] While we might agree with Lewis's efforts to alter public perceptions, it is possible that decriminalizing, or at least condoning, streaking presents its own problems. An acceptance of streaking would alter its readings, many of which centre on subverting law and authority and embracing the risqué and illicit. What might happen if streaking loses this substance? Legitimizing streaking might also lead to its proliferation and social apathy toward nudity. A point Carr-Gomm forewarns us of in his discussion on naked protest apathy.[46]

Streaking might remain marginalized, and its aesthetic conceptualizations in sport limited, yet nude bodily discourse will still be shaped by social change. As such, what we might witness are gradual shifts in attitudes leading towards more organized and controlled, less sporadic, collective naked practices. There are perhaps some signs of this in relation to the increasing popularity of nude rugby; a sport that, in comparison to the swifter and more furtive practice of streaking, presents ample opportunities for aesthetic performances. In New Zealand, nude rugby has become not only a novel sporting spectacle but also an enjoyable social display of bodies. The support the Nude Blacks get during their performances suggests that there is an acceptance, and appreciation, of beautiful bodies that transcends the conventionally costumed sporting participants. In Figure 7, we see not just a rugby moment but a merging of bodies, four of which huddle together to form a base, their heads tilted back, looking skyward. They support two other bodies with arms outstretched, reaching for the ball that eludes their grasp. The whole group is outlined against a seascape, echoing fine Greek or Roman sculpture, their collective physical contortions reminding us of the pleasures and pains of the body's physical experiences.

FIGURE 6.    *Lisa Lewis and the Commercial Corporeal.* Despite partial costuming, inveterate streaker Lisa Lewis is removed from the field during an All Blacks versus Ireland rugby match, July 2006

© *Sunday Star Times (Fairfax Media)*

FIGURE 7.    *The Beauty of the Form,* Dunedin's Nude Blacks. Acclaimed Nude Rugby Team strike a dynamic pose on the shore of St Kilda Beach, Dunedin, NZ, 2008

© *Fairfax Media*

CONCLUSION

It is generally acknowledged that there is confusion about clothes. What to wear is a constant sartorial dilemma. Various active naturist movements in the UK and elsewhere are typically premised on establishing a safe commune for naked bodies.[47] Going without clothes, however, does not easily present a solution, though those participating in the practice of streaking are experimenting with ways that this might be so. Perhaps more so than for the clothed body, there is a dynamic interplay between the *action* of taking off one's clothes and running, and the *reaction* that this mobility produces. Streaking does illustrate, in its own exhibitionist manner, the vitality of the body in motion in a way that a body costumed in linen, cotton, polyester or acrylic cannot.

REFERENCES

[1] Richard Martin, 'The Deceit of Dress: Utopian Visions and the Arguments Against Clothing', *Utopian Studies*, 4 (1991), 79–84 (p. 84).
[2] Bill Kirkpatrick, '"It Beats Rocks and Tear Gas": Streaking and Cultural Politics in the Post-Vietnam Era', *Journal of Popular Culture*, 43 (2010), 1023–47 (p. 1023).
[3] Ruth Barcan, *Nudity: A Cultural Anatomy* (Oxford: Berg, 2004), pp. 187–88.

[4] Joanne Entwistle, *The Fashioned Body: Fashion, Dress and Modern Social Theory* (Cambridge, UK: Polity Press, 2000).

[5] Confidential participant reflection, International Olympic Academy, Ancient Olympia, Greece, October 2008.

[6] Barcan, *Nudity*, p. 188.

[7] Larissa Bonfante, 'Nudity as a Costume in Classical Art', *American Journal of Archaeology*, 94 (1989), 557, cited in Barcan, *Nudity*, p. 183.

[8] Barcan, *Nudity*, p. 2.

[9] Kenneth Clark, *The Nude: A Study in Ideal Form* (Harmondsworth: Penguin, 1956).

[10] Anne Hollander, *Seeing Through Clothes* (Berkeley: University of California Press, 1993).

[11] Barcan, *Nudity*, p. 33.

[12] Philip Carr-Gomm, *A Brief History of Nakedness* (London: Reaktion, 2010), p. 7.

[13] John Berger, *Ways of Seeing* (Harmondsworth: Penguin, 1972), cited in Carr-Gomm, *A Brief History of Nakedness*, pp. 7–8.

[14] For example, Paul Bindrim, 'A Report on a Nude Marathon: The Effect of Physical Nudity upon the Practice of Interaction in the Marathon Group', *Psychotherapy: Theory, Research and Practice*, 5 (1968), 180–88; John M. MacDonald, *Indecent Exposure* (Springfield, IL: Charles C. Thomas, 1973); James M. Toolan, M. Elkins and P. D'Encamacao, 'The Significance of Streaking', *Medical Aspects of Human Sexuality*, 8 (1974), 152–57; William A. Anderson, 'The Social Organization and Social Control of a Fad: Streaking on a College Campus', *Urban Life*, 6 (1974), 221–40; 'Blue Streaks', *Newsweek*, 4 February 1974, p. 63; 'Columbia Campus Gets its First Gawk at "Streaking" Fad', *New York Times*, 7 March 1974, p. 41; Robert D. McFadden, 'Streaking: A Mad Dash to Where?', *New York Times*, 8 March 1974, pp. 35 and 41; Les Brown, 'TV Networks Seek to Avoid Streaking Incidents', *New York Times*, 29 March 1974, p. 71; 'The Founding Streakers', *Newsweek*, 20 May 1974, p. 120.

[15] Toolan et al., 'The Significance of Streaking'.

[16] Toolan et al., 'The Significance of Streaking', pp. 152–57 (p. 157).

[17] Carr-Gomm, *A Brief History of Nakedness*, p. 175.

[18] *Embodiment and Experience*, ed. by Theresa M. Csordas (Cambridge: Cambridge University Press, 1994); Caroline Fusco, 'Lesbians and Locker Rooms: The Subjective Experience of Lesbians in Sport', in *Sport and Postmodern Time*, ed. by Genevieve Rail (New York: SUNY, 1998); Kyle Kusz, 'BMX, Extreme Sports and the White Male Backlash', in *To The Extreme*, ed. by Rob Rinehart and Synthia Sydnor (New York: SUNY, 2003).

[19] Most notably, Allen Guttman, *The Erotic in Sports* (New York: Columbia University Press, 1996), but also Caroline Daley, *Leisure and Pleasure: Reshaping and Revealing the New Zealand Body* (Auckland: Auckland University Press, 2003); Frederick Schiff, 'Nude Dancing: Scenes of Sexual Celebration in a Contested Culture', *Journal of American Culture*, 4 (1999), 9–16; Charlene Weaving, 'She Strips . . . She Scores! An Analysis of Women Athletes Posing Nude', paper presented at 33rd Annual Meeting of the International Association for the Philosophy of Sport, Olomouc, 15–18 September 2005; Jayne Caudwell and Ian Wellard, *Sport, Pleasure and the Erotic* (New York: Routledge, in press 2012).

[20] Barcan, *Nudity*, p. 3.

[21] 'Nude Women's Rugby Calendar Creates Stir', *Otago Daily Times* (online edition), 6 December 2010; 'Naked Marathon Runner Gets Tasered', *Sydney Morning Herald* (online edition), 5 May 2011; 'Tennis Court Streaker Hits the Wall', *Sydney Morning Herald* (online edition), 27 January 2011; 'Nude Blacks Keeping Uniform', *Otago Daily Times* (online edition), 1 June 2011.

[22] Barcan, *Nudity*, p. 17.

[23] Barcan, *Nudity*; Florence Dee Boodakian, *Resisting Nudities: A Study in Aesthetics of Eroticism* (New York: Peter Lang, 2008); Carr-Gomm, *A Brief History of Nakedness*; Kirkpatrick, 'It Beats Rocks and Tear Gas'; Arnd Krüger, 'There Goes This Art of Manliness: Naturism and Racial Hygiene in Germany', *Journal of Sport History*, 18 (1991), 135–58; Stella Margetson, *Leisure and Pleasure in the Nineteenth Century* (London: Cassell, 1969); Chris Shilling, *Changing Bodies: Habit, Crisis and Creativity* (London: Sage, 2008); *Exposed: The Victorian Nude*, ed. by Alison Smith (New York: Watson-Guptill, 2002); Andrew F. Stewart, *Art, Desire and the Body in Ancient Greece* (Cambridge, UK: University of Cambridge Press, 1997).

[24] Entwistle, *The Fashioned Body*, p. 7.

[25] Barcan, *Nudity*, p. 16.

[26] Confidential participant reflection, oral interview, Knox College, Dunedin, New Zealand, 2010.

[27] Barcan, *Nudity*.

[28] Kirkpatrick, 'It Beats Rock and Tear Gas'.

[29] James W. Carey, 'Political Ritual on Television', in *Media, Ritual and Identity*, ed. by Tamar Liebes and James Curran (London and New York: Routledge, 1998), pp. 71–86; John Fiske, *Media Matters: Race and Gender in U.S. Politics* (Minneapolis: University of Minnesota Press, 1996).

[30] Kirkpatrick, 'It Beats Rock and Tear Gas'.

[31] Kirkpatrick, 'It Beats Rock and Tear Gas'.

[32] <http://www.stuff.co.nz/dominion-post/sport/sevens-2012/sevens-rugby/6366302/Pitch-invader-spoils-good-first-day-behaviour> [accessed 4 February 2012].

[33] Lewis Smith, 'Olympic Ban on Naked Commercialism', *The Independent* (online edition), 14 October 2011; Kurt Bayer, 'Trotting Cup Streaker Granted Diversion', *New Zealand Herald* (online edition), 25 November 2011; '"Seven" Streaker: "I didn't expect to tackle the guy but he had the ball"', *New Zealand Herald* (online edition), 8 February 2012.

[34] BBC editorial guidelines <http://www.bbc.co.uk/editorialguidelines/page/guidance-live-output-full> [accessed 4 February 2012].

[35] For instance, the 'breast not bombs' campaigners <http://breastnotbombs.blogspot.com>; the lengthy naked protest by working-class Mexicans <http://news.bbc.co.uk/I/hi/world/americas/2966496.stm>; the streaking to raise awareness about consumption and oil dependency <www.worldnakedbikeride.org>; or businessman and former New Zealand sportsman, Marc Ellis's patronage of nude day, <http://www.stuff.co.nz/timaru-herald/636308/Turning-the-other-cheek-all-for-fun> [all accessed 4 February 2012].

[36] <http://www.gamblingonlinemagazine.com/interviews.php?articleID=94> and <http://news.bbc.co.uk/sport1/hi/rugby_union/international/2182817.stm> [both accessed 4 February 2012].

[37] <www.streakerama.com/intro.htm> cited in Carr-Gomm, *A Brief History of Nakedness*, p. 180.

[38] Carr-Gomm, *A Brief History of Nakedness*, p. 181.

[39] Guttman, *The Erotic in Sports*; Stewart, *Art, Desire and the Body in Ancient Greece*.

[40] Carr-Gomm, *A Brief History of Nakedness*, p. 177.

[41] <http://www.womenstreakers.com/various3/var3.html> and <http://www.chinahush.com/2011/10/10/chinese-public-condemns-streaking-relay-as-vulgar-and-shameless/> [both accessed 4 February 2012].

[42] Caudwell and Wellard, *Sport, Pleasure and the Erotic*.

[43] Carr-Gomm, *A Brief History of Nakedness*, p. 179.

[44] <http://www.stuff.co.nz/sport/photos/2719047/Sporting-streakers> and <http://www.espncricinfo.com/nzvpak2009/content/image/438202.html> [both accessed 4 February 2012].

[45] 'Bikini Streaker Speaks Up For Tradition', *New Zealand Herald* (online edition), 18 May 2007.

[46] Carr-Gomm, *A Brief History of Nakedness*, pp. 89–133.

[47] David Bell and Ruth Holliday, 'Naked as Nature Intended', *Body and Society*, 6 (2000), 127–40; Nina J. Morris, 'Naked in Nature: Naturism, Nature and the Senses in Early Twentieth-Century Britain', *Cultural Geographies*, 16 (2009), 283–308.

GEOFFERY KOHE is a Lecturer in Sport Studies and Sociology in the Institute of Sport and Exercise Science at the University of Worcester, UK. Dr Kohe gained his PhD from the University of Otago in Dunedin, New Zealand. His thesis presented an historical account of the Olympic movement in New Zealand, and he was commissioned by the Olympic Committee of New Zealand to write an official history of that country's involvement in Olympic Games. His research interests include the socio-cultural, historical and political aspects of the Olympic movement, moral pedagogy, the politicizations of the body and sport tourism.

*Costume*, vol. 46, no. 2, 2012

# 'Hand of God', Shirt of the Man:
# The Materiality of Diego Maradona

By John Hughson *and* Kevin Moore

*Among the 'first eleven' items of interest in the National Football Museum, Manchester, UK is the football shirt worn by Diego Maradona (b. 1960) in the 1986 FIFA World Cup quarter-final match between Argentina and England. This paper reflects upon the cultural significance of the shirt as a museum object. A discussion of the shirt's history, from its wearing at the 1986 match to its imminent reappearance in the National Football Museum's new location, leads to the conclusion that, above all, although it may be subject to differing symbolic interpretations, the shirt exists as a material object, the observation of which affords football aesthetes an appreciative reminder of Maradona's extraordinary artistry with a ball at his feet.*

KEYWORDS: *football artistry, football shirt, Maradona, materiality, National Football Museum*

INTRODUCTION

When the Argentine Football Club, Boca Juniors, touted the idea of changing the design of their team's long-established playing strip, a most important voice was raised in protest. Diego Maradona, Boca Juniors' and Argentina's most famous football player of all time, declared that a market-driven incentive for profit from the sales of a new team strip should not prevail over the traditions of a football club, which symbolically reside in the shirt familiar to and loved by the fans.[1] With this gesture, Maradona indicated his awareness of the cultural importance of the football shirt. This paper pursues that theme in relation to one particular football shirt, the shirt worn by Maradona when playing for Argentina against England during the 1986 FIFA (International Federation of Association Football) World Cup Finals. It is now, courtesy of its owner, former England player Steve Hodge, located as a display item in the National Football Museum (Figures 1A and 1B).

The paper proceeds with a discussion of how key items of popular culture can be regarded in a similar fashion to museum items that have a 'high culture' status. The discussion then moves to an explanation of how an object analysis can be applied to Maradona's shirt. The final part of the object analysis, 'significance', then becomes the focus of the paper. At this point we examine the shirt in relation to the two goals scored by Maradona during the game in which it was worn. We indicate that the symbolic meaning of the shirt will vary according to the interpretations placed on it by viewers. These interpretations will often be derived from socio/political orientations. The paper concludes by positing that acknowledgement

     DOI: 10.1179/0590887612Z.00000000010

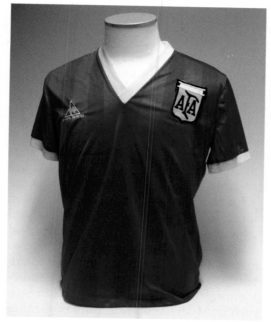

FIGURE IA. Football shirt, polyester, manufactured by Le Coq Sportif, 1986, front view. Worn by Diego Maradona at the 1986 FIFA World Cup quarter-final match, Argentina v. England. National Football Museum, Manchester UK (E561/ L119)
*Courtesy of the National Football Museum*

FIGURE IB. Diego Maradona's shirt, showing the number 10 printed in gold on the back
*Courtesy of the National Football Museum*

of such difference need not preclude an aesthetic awareness of the shirt's significance as a *material* reminder of Maradona as one of football's great artists.

## POPULAR BUT NOT ORDINARY: THE REVALUATION OF CULTURAL OBJECTS

In the book *Museums and Popular Culture*, one of the present authors considers how historians can explore and understand the significance of items of popular culture.[2] Objects from daily life, including many examples of dress, are displayed in a range of institutions and are studied by historians, as well as social anthropologists and ethnographers, in order to understand, almost literally, the material existence of civilizations from the distant and recent past.

Such display and enquiry can be rich and insightful in what it tells us about the history of social life, but necessarily tends to be objective rather than subjective. It often cannot get beneath the external layer of existence to look at the lives of ordinary people from their experiential perspective. This is where the term popular culture comes into play. Traditionally, culture has been the preserve of the aristocracy and upper classes and the cultural institutions of western nations still carry the mark of elitism. The notion of high culture has, of course, been under challenge for some time and this is reflected in the changing exhibition content of museums. In the summer of 2011, the Birmingham City Museum and Art Gallery featured an exhibition, including items of dress, on heavy metal music and its subculture. It is unlikely that such an exhibition in a museum of fine Victorian pedigree would have been countenanced a decade or so ago. And it is within the same timeframe that museums dedicated to popular culture and its particular forms — such as the National Football Museum, discussed in this paper — have opened to the public.

Against the weight of historical bias, museums of popular culture are as serious in intent as museums and galleries of so-called high culture. The changing nature of the academy and its impact on public debates about what constitutes culture has been beneficial to the legitimization of museums of popular culture within the museum sector. A key academic domain in this regard is the field of Cultural Studies, formally constituted within the academy in 1964 at the University of Birmingham.[3] Although Cultural Studies has, rather unfortunately, given rise to some of the most opaque and possibly gratuitous theorizing known to western scholarship, it has, despite its intellectual excesses, helped to substantially democratize the scholarly treatment of culture. Cultural Studies scholarship has articulated with other areas within the academy such as Media and Film Studies, Gender Studies and Dress Studies to validate intellectual investigation into various types and aspects of popular culture. In relation to museums, Cultural Studies has been extremely influential on what is referred to as the 'new museology'.[4] Cultural Studies is well known for its focus on the everyday life of ordinary people, but this does not mean an exclusive interest in ordinary items and artefacts. On the contrary, items of extraordinary appeal are placed very much on the agenda of research — and on display in museums — as such items within popular culture take on the same status as revered artworks within high culture.

How may the football shirt be so considered? As noted recently by sociologists Kendall and Osbaldiston, the football shirt is invested with considerable 'totemic power'.[5] It may be an everyday piece of clothing, quite literally so. A stroll on any given day along a high street in Britain will reveal young men, and often women, wearing the shirt of club or country.[6] But it is highly likely that the football shirt will carry a considerably greater significance for a person deeply enthusiastic about football than other garments they may routinely wear. Wearing the shirt is arguably the main way in which a fan can maintain a symbolic and, indeed, material identification with a professional club or national football team. This connection of football supporters to the shirt places a heavy onus on footballers to live up to the expectation that they must in all ways honour the shirt while playing for the team. Kendall and Osbaldiston note a number of examples from professional football of the pejorative phrase, 'you're not fit to wear the shirt', being used in criticism of players deemed to have failed in that duty. By contrast, players who are deemed to have performed heroically heighten the power of the shirt's significance, leading to its shrine-like preservation in trophy and paraphernalia rooms, football club museums, or even public museums, such as the National Football Museum.

The football shirt of Maradona at the centre of the discussion in this paper is a rather special object of this kind. It is not just one of Maradona's football shirts; it is a shirt worn during one of his most famous football-playing performances (Figure 2). The shirt allows us to remember not only Maradona, but also an historical sporting occasion in which he was the leading protagonist. That the game in question contained great controversy, at Maradona's instigation, has impacted upon the way the shirt will be interpreted by those who give it their attention. Such possibilities are outlined as the paper proceeds. The method of object analysis applied to Maradona's shirt is similar to that used by Moore in his analysis of another famous item associated with association football, and also located at the National Football Museum, the one remaining football from the 1966 FIFA World Cup Finals championship deciding match between England and Germany, played at Wembley Stadium.[7] Amongst other points of historical interest, the 1966 football and its story is hugely revealing, for example, of the post-war relations between England and Germany.[8]

The 1966 football is just one object from over 140,000 items in the collections of the National Football Museum. The analysis of the ball demonstrated the possibilities of material culture analysis of other key objects, in terms of what they can reveal about historical moments and the place of sport within history and also, to connect back to the discussion above, of how important sport is within people's lives. Yet, while politics and its ideologies, such as nationalism, are of great relevance to the interpretation of and debate over items like the 1966 football, these matters should not override the sense in which the ball holds an almost aesthetic significance for football lovers by providing lasting material evidence of a great match in a way that even film of the game cannot. It is in this latter sense that an

FIGURE 2. Maradona, on the right, reaches the ball before the English goalkeeper, Peter Shilton, but with a punch rather than a header. The resultant goal becomes famous as the 'Hand of God'.

© *Mirrorpix*

item of extraordinariness holds its cultural value to those devotees of a particular popular cultural form, in this case the sport of association football.

CUT FROM A DIFFERENT CLOTH: AN OBJECT ANALYSIS OF MARADONA'S SHIRT

The analysis of the 1966 World Cup football proceeded under the following headings: Description, Identification, Construction, History, Location, Distribution and Significance.[9] The present study of Maradona's shirt will use a slightly revised version of this structure, using the heading *Manufacture* instead of *Construction*. The brief entries under most headings are explanatory, the majority of discussion, involving the analytical dimension of the paper, occurs under the heading *Significance*.

## Description

The football shirt in question is that worn by Diego Maradona on 22 June 1986 in the quarter-final match of the 13th FIFA World Cup played in Mexico City, between Argentina and England. Maradona was the captain of Argentina. The shirt features the 'away strip' of Argentina, as Argentina assumed the 'away team' status for this particular game. A sequence of vertical stripes appears around the shirt in two similar shades of dark blue, difficult to differentiate at a distance. The shirt, then, is not of a type in keeping with the more familiar Argentina 'home strip', featuring a shirt with a two-stripe sequence of pale blue and white.

## Identification

The Maradona shirt is formally recorded in the National Football Museum as follows:

Entry Form Number E561; Loan Number L119; registered on Tuesday 14 October 2003.
Measurements:       Width across shoulder — 370 mm
                    Waist — 325 mm
                    Width at hem — 360 mm
                    Length, neck to hem — 280 mm

The shirt, like most others from this period, is made from a polyester fabric. Its condition is described within the records of the National Football Museum as 'match worn', with staining around the neck and on its short sleeves. Apart from that, the shirt is described as being in very good condition. It has no obvious markings to visually indicate that it was the shirt worn by Maradona on this occasion. The shirt's owner, Steve Hodge, claims that the shirt has not been laundered since it was handed to him in 1986 by Maradona himself.[10] Assuming this to be true, modern forensic tests, if applied, may be able to confirm that the shirt was either worn by or came into physical contact with the body of Diego Maradona.

## Manufacture

The manufacturer and supplier of the national team strip for Argentina at the time of the 1986 World Cup finals was Le Coq Sportif, a French firm founded in 1882 with the rooster logo added in 1948. The shirts for this tournament were the first to be worn by the Argentina football team to carry an emblem other than the national crest. While that emblem appeared familiarly on the left chest side of the shirt, the right chest side carried the Le Coq Sportif brand logo, featuring a rooster inside a triangle (Figure 1A). As one amongst several shirts produced for the Argentina team, the shirt's provenance in association with Maradona depends on it carrying the number 10, for which he was unrivalled in the Argentina team at the time (Figure 1B). We assume that Le Coq Sportif applied the numbers to the shirts, and each squad player — including Maradona — would have had several shirts with his number prepared in advance of the tournament.

*History*

Within this context, the history of the Maradona shirt refers to its state of existence from the time Maradona parted with it up to its present location in the National Football Museum. Following the World Cup quarter-final match in 1986, Maradona exchanged shirts in the customary fashion with England player Steve Hodge.

For this background on the shirt's history we are reliant on the account provided by Hodge: 'I'd kept all my England World Cup shirts, but as we were out [eliminated from the tournament after losing to Argentina] I decided to try and swap one. I went over to shake Maradona's hand [...] he was being mobbed by people and it was bedlam all around and I didn't bother. I just wished him all the best and walked away'. But then in the tunnel leaving the playing area they happened to make contact and the shirt swap occurred. According to Hodge, this is what happened: 'We looked at each other and I tugged at my shirt. He nodded and so I did, it was pure chance'.[11] Hodge retained the shirt in his home from 1986 until 2003 when he placed it on permanent loan under the care of the National Football Museum so that it could go on public display.

*Location*

The popularity of the shirt as a display item has resulted in its being chosen for the 'First Eleven', a leaflet pointing out to visitors the location of the eleven most requested pieces on display within the previous National Football Museum site (eleven, of course, being the number of players in a football team). The shirt has travelled since it came into the Museum's possession. When Steve Hodge's autobiography, *The Man with Maradona's Shirt*, was published in May 2010, the shirt was taken by National Football Museum staff to the book launch at a Waterstone's bookshop in London (Figure 3). It provided an opportunity (which may become rarer as the shirt is embedded into the handling and conservation practices of the museum) for the public to see the iconic object up-close and uncased. At the time of writing, November 2011, the Maradona shirt is on display at Nottingham Castle Museum. It has been in this location since the closure of the National Football Museum's Preston site at Deepdale Football Stadium since May 2010. With the

FIGURE 3.   Steve Hodge, the present owner of the shirt and a player in the 1986 game, holds up the Maradona shirt at a book launch in 2010

*Courtesy of the National Football Museum*

reopening of the National Football Museum in May 2012 at its new Manchester site, the Urbis building, the shirt will return as one of the star exhibits.

## Distribution

The 'authentic' Maradona shirt under discussion is obviously out of commercial circulation. However, its owner Steve Hodge indicated in an interview in 2010 that he believes the shirt would fetch in the order of £200,000 at auction, should he be disposed to sell it.[12] He bases this estimate on an auction sale of a shirt worn by Pelé (Edson Arantes do Nascimento, b. 1940) in the 1970 World Cup Final. In regard to the mass market, 'replica' Maradona shirts are readily available from online purchase sites. This includes replicas advertised as the 'Argentina 1986 World Cup Away Maradona No. 10 Shirt'. The product description identifies the shirt as a replica of that worn by Maradona in the game against England. One example of such a shirt, claimed by its seller to be signed by Maradona, is available for sale on eBay, at the time of writing, at the cost of £149.99.[13]

## Significance

To investigate the significance of an object we must question its symbolic importance stemming from its material condition and, where applicable, ask whether the object symbolically transcends those conditions. The discussion of Maradona's shirt in the remaining section of this paper will take us into both areas of enquiry in turn. The museum theorist Susan Pearce contends that 'objects make history'.[14] In the case of Maradona's shirt, the meanings invested in it provide for a re-imagining of the past: the 1986 Argentina/England game within a much broader social and political context. To make further sense of this claim it is necessary to provide some details of that World Cup quarter-final match, played on 22 June 1986 in Mexico City.

As a quarter-final, the game had 'sudden death' status, with the winning team advancing to the semi-finals and the losing team being eliminated from the tournament. This alone was enough to ensure that the contest was filled with tension and keen rivalry, but at least two other factors, one directly linked to football, the other at a remove from sport, had further bearing on the game's intensity. Firstly, Argentina and England had developed a reputation as hostile rivals in international football, tracing back to the 1966 World Cup when, again in the quarter-finals, they faced each other.[15] The Argentina players turned to aggressive play, so much so that the England manager Sir Alf Ramsay accused them of behaving like 'animals' and refused to allow his players to engage in the customary shirt swapping between opponents after a final. A well-known photograph shows him stepping between Nobby Stiles and an Argentine player to prevent an exchange being made. Three intervening friendly matches notwithstanding, the 1986 quarter-final was the first meeting between Argentina and England in a football game of competitive status since the 1966 encounter.

Beyond matters of football, but certainly not international hostility, the 1986 World Cup quarter-final was the first time that Argentina had played against England since the Falklands or Malvinas War of 1982.[16] A special effort was made at the time by the football authorities to downplay any political or jingoistic rivalry ahead of the game. The players of the respective teams were incorporated into this agenda and Maradona, as captain of Argentina, promulgated the official line on the match being totally about football and not politics. However, his subsequent pronouncements indicate that this was just a mask of public relations. Recanting the comment he made in 1986 that the game was to be played like any other, Maradona, in his autobiography, declares 'it was not just another match [. . .] it was revenge'. And given that the Argentina team prevailed in the match, he was able to add, 'it was like recovering a little bit of the Malvinas'.[17] As scorer of the two Argentina goals in the game — two of the most famous goals in the history of football — his role in this 'recovery' was paramount. The very different nature of these goals and their contestable symbolic interpretation provide the allure, as a museum attraction, of the shirt worn by Maradona during their scoring (Figure 4).[18]

## MAKING HISTORY, MAKING ART: THE MEANINGS AND AESTHETICS OF MARADONA'S SHIRT

The 1966 World Cup ball has been called a 'polysemantic' object; it can mean different things to different people.[19] It might also suggest that the ball means different things to the same person. Alternative and alternating possibilities of interpretation apply to Maradona's shirt. Can we perhaps regard the shirt in the way that Salazar-Sutil has written of Maradona himself as 'a mirror on which anyone can project an image or signification'?[20] The answer is almost but not quite,

FIGURE 4. Maradona, running second from left, scores the second goal, the 'Goal of the Century'
©*Mirrorpix*

as there is a key difference between the shirt and the man whom Salazar-Sutil aptly refers to as 'Maradona Inc.': the global brand that Maradona has become via a series of shifting and contradictory (non-sporting) performances over the years. Within this frame Maradona is more a mirage than a man of flesh and bone. But, while Maradona the person has become larger than life, material items of his past allow us to recall the man that he was. Accordingly, his shirt, ostensibly a fairly ordinary garment, is a material reminder that Maradona the football player, who scored those goals against England in 1986, really did exist.

For some English people the shirt is a material reminder of their national team being cheated out of an opportunity to progress towards a World Cup final. This lingering attitude prompts reflection upon the appropriateness of the shirt being held and displayed in England's national museum of football. As recently as 2008, Terry Butcher, a defensive player for England in the 1986 match, and a later captain of the national team, reacted angrily when questioned by the media about the Maradona shirt. Butcher was antagonistic enough to declare that he would not even use it to wash his car, an unintended comment on the ease with which garments, rather more than any other artefacts, can be recycled.[21] Butcher's opinion evokes England's old Corinthian football culture, within which cheating is regarded as an intolerable treachery against the game itself. But, as noted by a number of commentators, including Maradona's biographer Jimmy Burns, obeying the rules of the game is not a universal ethic, and, indeed, successfully defying the rules can be regarded admirably within Argentina's football culture.[22] Certain circumstances can heighten a favourable response to rule-breaking, and such is the case with Maradona's 'Hand of God' goal to some nationalistic Argentines. According to Albarces and Rodriguez, the goal 'can be read as a piece of Creole knavery against

[29] Alan Hudson, *The Working Man's Ballet* (London: Robson Books, 1998). The aesthetic capacity in football was recognized in 2008 by the English National Ballet (ENB). To mark the eighty-fifth anniversary of the founding of the Littlewoods Football Pools, the ENB choreographed and performed the re-enactment of ten moments from football history, including Maradona's 'hand of God' goal. Former England player John Barnes remarked, 'this ballet is a celebration of two beautiful arts that are more alike than you might think'. <http://www.telegraph.co.uk/culture/theatre/dance/3560268/The-Beautiful-Game-the-English-National-Ballet-brings-football-to-the-stage.html> [accessed 30 November 2011].

[30] The projected annual attendance figure for the National Football Museum in its Manchester, Urbis Building location is 350,000. National Football Museum: Business Plan, 1 April 2011–31 March 2016.

JOHN HUGHSON is Professor of Sport and Cultural Studies at the University of Central Lancashire. He is the author of *The Making of Sporting Cultures* (2009) and principal author of *The Uses of Sport* (2005). Among other projects, he is presently researching the cultural and historical significance of Olympic Games posters. A case-study of Richard Beck's poster for the Melbourne 1956 Olympic Games is to appear in a forthcoming issue of the *Journal of Design History*. Hughson is Chair of the Academic Advisory Panel to the National Football Museum.

KEVIN MOORE is Director of the National Football Museum, a post he has held since the inception of the Museum project in 1997. From 1992 to 1997 he was a Lecturer in Museum Management and Marketing at the Department of Museum Studies, University of Leicester, UK. He has published a number of academic works on museums, including *Museums and Popular Culture* (1997), *Management in Museums* (1999) and *Museum Management* (1994). He is co-editor of the forthcoming book *Sport, History and Heritage: An Investigation into the Public Representation of Sport*. Moore is Chair of the Sports Heritage Network, the organization of the UK's sports museums. In 2008 he was elected a Fellow of the RSA.

*Costume*, vol. 46, no. 2, 2012

# Dressed for Sport: A Photographic Miscellany

*Compiled by* PENELOPE BYRDE

When we were preparing the June 2012 issue of *Costume* on the theme of sports-wear, the Editors invited some UK museums to submit photographs of relevant objects in their collections. We hope that this selection may be of interest to readers.

## THE WENLOCK OLYMPIAN SOCIETY HERALD

FIGURE 1. The Herald's costume

    DOI: 10.1179/174963012X13319136517511

The Wenlock Olympian Society was formed in 1850 to promote Olympian Games for all and attracted competitors from all over the country. The WOS Games inspired Baron de Coubertin, following a visit to Much Wenlock, to form the International Olympian Committee. The mascot for London 2012 is called Wenlock after the Society's history, and Jonathan Edwards is the WOS President.

The Herald led the procession to the WOS Games ground. The WOS founder, William Penny Brookes, wrote to Covent Garden regarding what a herald might wear and this is the result of their advice. The costume has just been conserved for redisplay in the renovated Much Wenlock Museum ready for 2012.
**www.muchwenlockmuseum.co.uk**

## ROWING COLOURS

Ian Whitehead, Keeper of Maritime History at Tyne and Wear Archives and Museums, wrote about some of the silk handkerchiefs that were produced as 'colours' for professional rowing races in the latter half of the nineteenth century:

Rowing colours took the form of a large silk handkerchief, printed with a commemorative design. The issuing of colours worked in a similar way to the marketing of football strips today, and provided a useful secondary income for oarsmen. Colours were designed and offered for sale whenever there was a major race. The usual charge for the handkerchief was 1 guinea (£1. 1s.). Nine of these 'colours' handkerchiefs, approximately a yard square and dating from 1869 to 1895, are in this collection.

James Renforth, World Sculling Champion, is shown stripped to the waist with one of these colours tied round his neck. He died soon after collapsing during a race in Canada in 1871 (when the photograph was taken) and was buried wearing the colour issued for that race.

**www.twmuseums.org.uk**

FIGURE 2.   Rowing colour, 1895

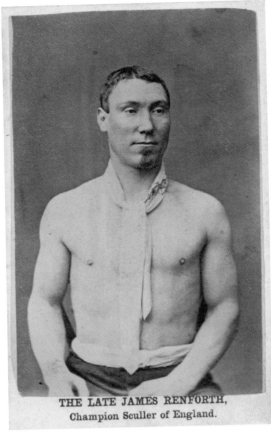

THE LATE JAMES RENFORTH,
Champion Sculler of England.

FIGURE 3.   James Renforth, 1871

FIGURE 4.   Detail of border
of colour, 1895

**HOCKEY**

FIGURE 5.   English women's hockey team, 1899
*National Hockey Museum*

**www.hockeyarchives.co.uk**

**BADMINTON**

FIGURE 6.   Badminton match, *c.* 1910

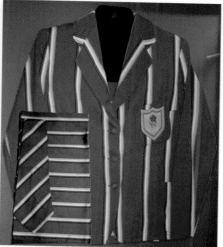

FIGURE 7.   Blazer, scarf and tie, 1904
*National Badminton Museum*

**www.badmintonengland.co.uk**

**SPORTS SHOES** — From the Shoe Collection at Northampton Museums and Art Gallery

FIGURE 8.   Pair of women's *Ubique* tennis shoes with their original box, by William Hickson & Sons, c. 1897. Leather and rubber. 1975.144.67P. Purchased from D. Holtom

© *NMAG*

FIGURE 9.   Pair of women's bar-style tennis shoes by Renshaw, 1900–1920. Glacé leather and rubber. 1985.159.2. Gift of D. M. Taylor

© *NMAG*

FIGURE 10.   Pair of boy's sports boots by Mobbs and Co. Ltd, 1902–1910. Canvas and rubber. 1972.8.14P. Purchased from D. Faulkner.

© *NMAG*

FIGURE 11.   Pair of men's sports shoes, c. 1920. Leather, canvas and rubber. 1972.60.8. Transfer from Portsmouth Museum

© *NMAG*

FIGURE 12. Man's running spike by Adidas, 1955. Goatskin. Worn by Sir Christopher Chattaway when he completed a four-minute mile (3 min 58 sec) at the White City Stadium on 28 May 1955 (14 sec slower than Roger Bannister on 6 May 1954). 1973.89.34. Gift of Northampton College of Technology
© *NMAG*

FIGURE 13. Pair of women's ten-pin bowling shoes, by Brunswick, 1965. Rubber and leather. Worn by Linda Hood at Northampton's first ten-pin bowling alley (Fairlanes), Weedon Road. 2001.71. Gift of Linda Hood
© *NMAG*

FIGURE 14. Man's motor racing boot, by C. E. Lewis, 1979–1980. Canvas and leather. Worn by Emerson Fittipaldi. 1982.112.3. Gift of Edward Lewis
© *NMAG*

**www.northampton.gov.uk**

**FENCING**

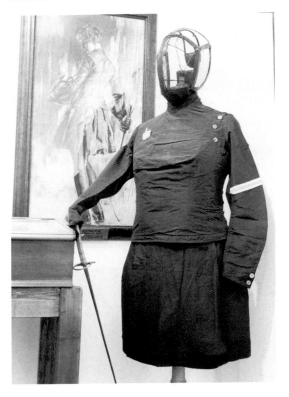

FIGURE 15.   Woman's silk fencing outfit, Victorian
*National Fencing Museum*

FIGURE 16.   Fencing master's jacket, sailcloth and suede, late nineteenth century
*National Fencing Museum*

**www.nationalfencingmuseum.com**

RUGBY

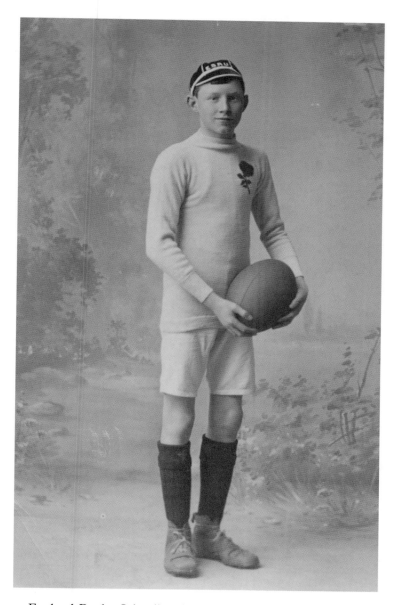

FIGURE 17.   England Rugby Schoolboy jersey, *c.* 1905. A postcard of an English Rugby Union Schoolboy International. At this time England rugby jerseys were made from wool. By 1914 woollen jerseys had been replaced by cotton, the material having been found to retain less water on wet and muddy rugby pitches

*World Rugby Museum*

**www.rfu.com/museum**

FIGURE 18.   Rugby shirt dress, made from recycled rugby shirts, by Gary Harvey, 2008. The Bath rugby team home kit by Puma, 2011, is worn by players Francois Louw, Matt Carraro and Nathan Catt. Gary Harvey's rugby shirt dress is one of the exhibits in the *Sport and Fashion* exhibition at the Fashion Museum, Bath (from February 2012) (**www.museumofcostume.co.uk**). It is an example of the designer's success in 'eco-fashion'. Harvey's technique of using discarded clothing as the basis of his work has won many admirers, including Livia Firth, wife of the actor Colin Firth, who paraded Gary Harvey's creations on the red carpet at last year's Oscar and Bafta award ceremonies (**www.garyharvey.creative.com**). Photographer: Colin Hawkins.
Model: Fiona at Gingersnap

© *Fashion Museum, Bath & North East Somerset Council*

*Costume*, vol. 46, no. 2, 2012

# Retrospective List of Articles on Sportswear Published in *Costume* 1968–2008

*Compiled by* PAT POPPY

Rebecca Arnold, 'Modern Fashions for Modern Women: The Evolution of New York Sportswear in the 1930s', 41 (2007), 111–25.

Cally Blackman, 'Walking Amazons: The Development of the Riding Habit in England during the Eighteenth Century', 35 (2001), 47–58.

Ella Bland, 'Family Motoring in Edwardian Times', 29 (1995), 114.

Nancy Bradfield, 'Cycling in the 1890s', 6 (1972), 3–47. Article based on letters and papers of S. S. Buckman.

Anne Buck, 'Foundations of the Active Woman in *La Belle Epoque Costume 1890–1914*' (Proceedings of the First Annual Conference of the Costume Society, 1967), (1968), 43–48. The changes made in women's clothing by women taking up sport in the period 1890–1910.

J. Burnett and J. Griffiths, 'Early Protective Clothing in Cricket', 19 (1985), 110–20.

Penelope Byrde, '"That Frightful Unbecoming Dress": Clothes for Spa Bathing at Bath', 21 (1987), 44–56.

Penelope Byrde and Peter Brears, 'A Pair of James I's Gloves', 24 (1990), 34–42. Describes a pair of early seventeenth-century gauntlet gloves which may have been worn for riding or hunting.

Irene Foster, 'The Development of Riding Costume c.1880–1920', 3 (1969), 55–60.

Catherine Horwood, '"Anyone for Tennis?": Male Dress and Decorum on the Tennis Courts in Inter-War Britain', 38 (2004), 100–05.

Lucy Johnston, 'She and Ski: The Development of Women's Ski Outfits, 1880–1930', 38 (2004), 86–99.

Diana Rait Kerr, 'The Costume of a Cricketer', 7 (1973), 50–54.

Claudia Kidwell, 'Apparel for Ballooning with Speculations on More Commonplace Garb', 11 (1977), 73–87. The costume worn by Dr John Jefferies while ballooning in 1785.

Avril Lansdell, 'Costume for Oarswomen, 1919–1979', 13 (1979), 73–79.

DOI: 10.1179/174963012X13319136517313

Jane Malcolm-Davies, '"And at the Plastron Push": The Historical Development of Fencing Kit', 36 (2002), 100–11. The article focuses on the specialized garments developed for the sport of foil fencing from the late sixteenth century to the First World War.

Alan Mansfield, 'Blazers', 5 (1971), 25–28. Tracing their origins in rowing and cricket clubs in the mid-nineteenth century.

Deirdre Murphy, '"Stylish Yet Perfectly Modest": Women's Bathing Dress in England, 1850–1900', 38 (2004), 63–71.

Deirdre Murphy, '"The Girls in Green": Women's Seaside Dress in England', 40 (2006), 56–66.

Susan North, 'John Redfern and Sons, 1847–1892', 42 (2008), 145–68. Includes discussion of women's tailor-made costumes by Redfern for riding, travelling, walking and yachting.

Richard Rutt, 'The Englishman's Swimwear', 24 (1990), 69–84.

Kate Strasdin, '"An Easy Day for a Lady": The Dress of Early Women Mountaineers', 38 (2004), 72–85. The article investigates the dress of women mountaineers from 1850 to 1914.

*Costume*, vol. 46, no. 2, 2012

# New and Recent Books

*Compiled by* Anna Buruma

*A Perfect Fit: The Garment Industry and American Jewry 1860–1960*, ed. by Gabriel Goldstein and Elizabeth Greenberg (Texas Tech University Press, 2012). 264 pp., 151 col. illus. $34.97. ISBN: 978-0-89672-735-9.

Heather M. Akou, *The Politics of Dress in Somali Culture* (Indiana University Press, 2011). 200 pp., 30 b/w illus., 1 map. £16.99. ISBN: 978-0-253-22313-5.

Jill D'Alessandro, *Pulp Fashion: The Art of Isabelle de Borchgrave* (Prestel, 2011). 104 pp., 87 col. illus. £19.99. ISBN: 978-3-7913-5105-6 (handcrafted paper fashions).

Cynthia Amnéus, Sara Long Butler and Katherine Jellison, *Wedded Perfection: Two Centuries of Wedding Gowns* (D. Giles, 2010). 196 pp., 136 col. & 21 b/w illus. £30.00. ISBN: 978-1-904832-843.

Miren Arzalluz, *Cristóbal Balenciaga: The Work of the Master* (V&A, 2011). 308 pp., 100 col. & 170 b/w illus. £30.00. ISBN: 9781851776634.

Alison Bancroft, *Fashion and Psychoanalysis: Styling the Self* (I. B. Taurus, 2012). 256 pp. £17.99 ISBN: 9781780760049.

Cristina Barreto and Martin Lancaster, *Napoleon and the Empire of Fashion 1795–1815* (Skira, 2011). £40.00. 208 pp. ISBN: 978-8857206509.

Djurdja Bartlett, *FashionEast: The Spectre that Haunted Socialism* (MIT Press, 2010). 300 pp., 70 col. & 96 b/w illus. £24.95. ISBN: 978-0262026505.

Linda Baumgarten, *What Clothes Reveal: The Language of Clothing in Colonial and Federal America*: The Colonial Williamsburg Collection (Yale University Press, 2012). 280 pp., 355 col. & 36 b/w illus. ISBN: 978-0300181074.

Ariel Beaujot, *Victorian Fashion Accessories* (Berg, 2011). 192 pp., 53 b/w illus. ISBN: 9781847886828.

Alison Behnke, *The Little Black Dress and Zoot Suits: Depression and Wartime Fashions from the 1930s to 1950s* (Twenty-First Century Books, 2011). 64 pp. £20.70. ISBN: 978-0-7613-5886-2.

*British Asian Style: Fashion and Textiles, Past and Present*, ed. by Christopher Breward, Philip Crang and Rosemary Crill (V&A, 2010). 208 pp., 180 col. illus. £24.99. ISBN: 9781851776191.

*British Design from 1948: Innovation in the Modern Age*, ed. by Christopher Breward and Ghislaine Wood (V&A, 2012). 350 pp., 350 col. illus. £40.00. ISBN: 9781851776740.

   DOI: 10.1179/174963012X13319136517359

Lisa Chaney, *Chanel: An Intimate Life* (Fig Tree, 2011). 512 pp., 59 illus. £25.00. ISBN: 978-1905490363.

*Colour Move: Art and Fashion by Sonia Delaunay*, ed. Matilda MacQuaid (Thames and Hudson, 2011). 204 pp. £22.50. ISBN: 978-0500289396.

Noel Cox, *Academical Dress in New Zealand: A Study* (VDM, 2010). 284 pp. £68.00. ISBN: 978-3639299274.

Elisabeth Crowfoot, Frances Pritchard and Kay Staniland, *Textiles and Clothing, c.1150–1450: Finds from Medieval Excavations in London (Medieval Finds from Excavations in London)* (Boydell Press, 2012, first published 2006). 223 pp. £19.99. ISBN: 978-1843832393.

Design Museum, *Fifty Bags that Changed the World* (Conran Octopus, 2011). 112 pp. £12.99. ISBN: 978-1840915709.

Design Museum, *Fifty Hats that Changed the World* (Conran Octopus, 2011). 112 pp. £12.99. ISBN: 978-1840915693.

Mairead Dunlevy, *Pomp and Poverty: A History of Silk in Ireland* (Yale University Press, 2011). 280 pp., 135 col. & 25 b/w illus. £45.00. ISBN: 9780300170412.

Eiluned Edwards, *Textiles and Dress of Gujarat* (V&A, 2011). 240 pp., 240 col. illus. £35.00. ISBN: 9781851776450.

Nina Edwards, *On the Button: The Significance of an Ordinary Item* (I. B. Taurus, 2012). 272 pp. £14.99. ISBN: 978-1848855847.

Tim Edwards, *Fashion in Focus: Concepts, Practices and Politics* (Kindle edition, 2011). 723 KB. £19.99. ASIN: B004OBZXNK.

Edwina Ehrman, *The Wedding Dress: 300 Years of Bridal Fashions* (V&A, 2011). 208 pp., 185 col. illus. £30.00. ISBN: 978-1851775064.

Bonnie English, *Japanese Fashion Designers: The Work and Influence of Issey Miyake, Yohji Yamamoto and Rei Kawakubo* (Berg, 2011). 192 pp. £17.99. ISBN: 978-1847883100.

Irene Favaretto and Isabella Campagnol, *Rubelli: The Art of Weaving* (Marsilio, 2012). 256 pp. £35.00. ISBN: 978-8831708227.

Lilli Fransen, Anna Norgard and Else Ostergard, *Medieval Garments Reconstructed: Norse Clothing Patterns* (Aarhus University Press, 2011). 143 pp. £25.00. ISBN: 978 87 7934 298 9.

John Block Friedman, *Brueghel's Heavy Dancers: Transgressive Clothing, Class, and Culture in the Late Middle Ages* (Medieval Studies, 2010). 456 pp. £39.95. ISBN: 978-0815632153.

Horst A. Friedrichs, *Cycle Style* (Prestel, 2012). 192 pp., 200 col. illus. £19.99. ISBN: 978-3-7913-4662-5.

Simon Gatrell, *Thomas Hardy Writing Dress* (Peter Lang, 2011). 298 pp., num. illus. £70.79. ISBN: 978-3034307390.

Pamela Church Gibson, *Fashion and Celebrity Culture* (Berg, 2011). 304 pp., 40 b/w & 24 col. illus. £16.99. ISBN: 9781847883865.

Peter Gonsalves, *Clothing for Liberation: A Communication Analysis of Gandhi's Swadeshi Revolution* (Sage Publications, 2010). 188 pp. £29.99. ISBN: 978-8132103103.

*Identities through Fashion*, ed. by Ana Marta Gonzales and Laura Bovone (Berg, 2012). 240 pp., 2 b/w illus. £19.99. ISBN: 978-0857850584.

Jerome Gautier, *Chanel: The Vocabulary of Style* (Thames & Hudson, 2011). 304 pp., 211 col. & b/w illus. £65.00. ISBN: 978-0500515815.

Adam Geczy and Vicki Karaminas, *Fashion and Art* (Berg, 2012). 224 pp., 32 col. & 5 b/w illus. £19.99. ISBN: 978-1847887832.

Rebecca Haidt, *Women, Work and Clothing in Eighteenth-Century Spain* (SVEC, Voltaire Foundation, 2011). 362 pp. £65.00. ISBN: 978-0729410229.

Joseph Harris, *Hidden Agendas: Cross-Dressing in Seventeenth-Century France* (Gunter Narr Verlag Tübingen, 2011). 279 pp. £42.93. ISBN: 978-3823361145.

Anat Helman, *A Coat of Many Colors: Dress Culture in the Young State of Israel* (Academic Studies Press, 2011). 300 pp. £45.95. ISBN: 978-1934843888.

Daniel Delis Hill, *American Menswear from the Civil War to the Twenty-First Century* (Texas Tech University Press, 2011). 376 pp. £51.95. ISBN: 978-0896727229.

Susan Hiner, *Accessories to Modernity: Fashion and the Feminine in Nineteenth-Century France* (University of Pennsylvania Press, 2010). 288 pp. £31.00. ISBN: 978-0812242591.

Hua Mei, *Chinese Clothing* (CUP, 2011). 170 pp. £12.99. ISBN: 978-0521186896.

*Hussein Chalayan*, ed. by Robert Violette (Rizzoli, 2011). £53.75. ISBN: 978-0847837311. (In French.)

Susan Ingram and Katrina Sark, *Berliner Chic: A Locational History of Berlin Fashion* (Intellect, 2010). 256 pp. £19.95. ISBN: 978-1841503691.

Andrew M. Ivaska, *Cultured States: Youth, Gender, and Modern Style in 1960s Dar es Salaam* (Duke University Press, 2011). 312 pp. £64.00. ISBN: 978-0822347491.

Helen Jennings, *New African Fashion* (Prestel, 2011). 240 pp., 250 col. illus. £19.99. ISBN: 978-3-7913-4696-0.

James H. Johnson, *Venice Incognito: Masks in the Serene Republic* (University of California Press, 2011). 316 pp. £27.95. ISBN: 978-0520267718.

Yuni Kawamura, *Doing Research in Fashion and Dress* (Berg, 2011). 192 pp. £17.99. ISBN: 978-1847885821.

Harold Koda and Andrew Bolton, *Schiaparelli and Prada: Impossible Conversations* (Yale University Press, 2012). 288 pp., 200 col. & b/w illus. $50.00. ISBN: 9780300179552.

Katherine Krohn, *Calico Dresses and Buffalo Robes: American West Fashions from the 1840s to 1890s* (Twenty-First Century Books, 2011). 64 pp. ISBN: 978-0761358909.

Roberta Orsi Landini, *Moda a Firenze 1540–1. Lo stile di Cosimo I de' Medici* (Mauro Pagliai, Florence, 2011). 312 pp. £82.39. Bilingual Italian and English text. ISBN: 978-8856400991 (companion volume by the same author to: *Moda a Firenze 1540-1580. Lo stile di Eleonora di Toledo e la sua influenza*, 2005).

Eve MacSweeney, *Nostalgia in Vogue* (Rizzoli, 2011). 336 pp. £35.00. ISBN: 978-0847836819.

*Medieval Clothing and Textiles*, 7, ed. by Robin Netherton and Gale R. Owen-Crocker (Boydell Press, 2011). 180 pp., illus. £30.00. ISBN: 9781843836254.

*Medieval Clothing and Textiles*, 8 ed. by Robin Netherton and Gale R. Owen-Crocker (Boydell Press, 2012). 172 pp., illus. £30.00. ISBN: 9781843837367.

Lynn A. Meisch and Ann Pollard Rowe, *Costume and History in Highland Ecuador* (University of Texas Press, 2011). 402 pp. £40.00. ISBN: 978-0292725911.

Daniel Miller and Sophie Woodward, *Blue Jeans: The Art of the Ordinary* (University of California Press, 2012). 168 pp. £41.95. ISBN: 978-0520272187.

Monica L. Miller, *Slaves to Fashion: Black Dandyism and the Styling of Black Diasporic Identity* (Duke University Press, 2010). 408 pp. £67.00. ISBN: 978-0822345855.

Bianca du Mortier and Ninke Bloemberg, *Accessorize! 250 Objects of Fashion and Desire* (Yale University Press, 2010). 272 pp. ISBN: 978-9086890453.

Lucy Norris, *Recycling Indian Clothing: Global Context of Reuse and Value* (Indiana University Press, 2010). 208 pp. £16.99. ISBN: 978-0253222084.

Susan North and Jenny Tiramani, *Seventeenth-Century Women's Dress Patterns: Bk 1* (V&A, 2011). 160 pp., 350 col. illus. £35.00. ISBN: 9781851776313.

Susan North and Jenny Tiramani, *Seventeenth-Century Women's Dress Patterns: Bk 2* (V&A, 2012). 160 pp., 400 col. illus. £35.00. ISBN: 9781851776856.

Simon Peers, *Golden Spider Silk* (V&A, 2012). 48 pp., 80 col. illus. £5.00. ISBN: 9781851777013.

*Peonies and Pagodas: Embroidered Parsi Textiles: TAPI Collection*, ed. by Shipla Shah and Tulsi Vatsa (Garden Silk Mills, 2010). 196 pp., col. illus. $61.46. ISBN: 9788190593519.

Aileen Ribeiro, *Facing Beauty: Painted Women and Cosmetic Art* (Yale University Press, 2011). 256 pp., 100 col. & 50 b/w illus. £30.00. ISBN: 978-0300124866.

A range of approaches are employed throughout: dress as object, dress in/as images, fashion in archives, fashion texts and documents, the 'people and places' of fashion, time and space and the role of cultural geography are all discussed, pointing up the multitude of methodological approaches that can be taken in investigating and researching fashion, costume and dress. Material and image analysis and oral history are particularly highlighted especially in relation to their use for the understanding of twentieth-century museums' dress or fashion collections, and the materiality of garments when integrated with archival, printed and representational sources is, the editors argue, a 'key methodological tool for the future history of fashion'. Explorations of modernity, class and gender are included throughout and, as a scholar particularly interested in the previously underexplored area of men and fashion (discussed here by Christopher Breward), it is good to see that explorations of men's fashion and masculinity are given a considerable presence.

Criticism could be directed at the fact that the balance is in favour of examples exploring western Europe. The editors recognize that there is relatively little material where serious scholars investigate beyond Euroamerica and they try to redress this imbalance through commissioned 'snapshots' and reading suggestions. Another area of possible improvement could be in the number of images; more is always desirable. However, this could be levelled at many academic-based fashion books and is often a result of limited funding rather than a lack of will or desire on the part of authors and editors. Overall this is an excellent volume which thoroughly earns its place both in the increasing library of fashion-related readers published over recent years and as a work which opens up the debate on fashion history. I would thoroughly recommend it to students, accomplished scholars and any readers interested in the continuing history of fashion.

SHAUN COLE
London College of Fashion

Hua Mei, *Chinese Clothing* (Cambridge and New York: Cambridge University Press, 2011). 170 pp., illus. throughout, chiefly col. Pbk £14.27. ISBN 9780521186896 and 0521186897.

*Chinese Clothing* is published in the Cambridge University Press *Introductions to Chinese Culture* series. Hua Mei is well qualified to give an overview of this broad topic: she has been writing on Chinese dress since the early 1990s, and her 2001 *Fushi yu Zhongguo wenhua* (*Dress and Chinese Culture*) is widely cited. Here Hua ambitiously endeavours to cover nearly all aspects of Chinese dress, and inevitably the result is quite uneven.

The first two chapters on historical dress, official and non-official, are largely successful and, given the scarcity of English-language works on the history of Chinese dress prior to the Qing dynasty (1644–1911), will be much welcomed. Hua presents an informed overview, indicating key social and cultural processes, but also giving the reader a flavour of the richness of literary descriptions, and the details of historical make-up and hairstyles. She illustrates thought-provoking interactions between Asian countries, in particular the influence wielded by Chinese styles. The reader is left with many questions: how did the 'open-minded, aristocratic women of the Tang' negotiate Confucian mores to dress with such abandon? Why were Ming women more reserved and subdued than their Tang counterparts? This should prompt many to further research, and it is unfortunate that there is no further reading listed.

The third chapter comprises a brief history of silk production and some of the associated folklore. Hua demonstrates the sophistication of the early weaving technologies, and briefly discusses cultural exchange on the Silk Road; the examples of foreign influence on Chinese textiles are particularly interesting as, for example, Han fabrics with Buddhist patterns or Greek mythological creatures.

In the subsequent chapters, the content becomes a little weaker and the presentation more sketchy. Readers new to the subject will have difficulty processing the largely unorganized and descriptive mass of information about the fifty-six official minorities groups living within China's borders. Hua attempts to encompass them all and is not helped by the absence of a map. She recounts evocative tales behind the clothing traditions but, by presenting the objects primarily in decorative terms, she often projects a demeaning image of minority people. For example, the colours of a Dulong blanket are described as 'primitive and simple'. There is little attempt to address the present-day economic and social identity of minorities, nor the effects of modernization upon dress culture.

The chapter on contemporary fashion is also problematic. Although it contains some striking illustrations, especially from the mid-twentieth century and Cultural Revolution period (1966–1976), the reader would have benefited from a discussion of the social and cultural mechanisms that have allowed Chinese consumers today to enjoy fashion (issues recently carefully considered by Wu Juanjuan, *Chinese Dress: From Mao to Now*, 2009). Noticeable omissions are the influence of pop and print culture, and that of Western luxury brands and styles from Taiwan and Japan. Also neglected here are the huge industrial changes — the transition from state-owned garment factories to private clothing producers — as well as changing conceptions of the fashion designer.

Given the ambitious coverage, the book suffers from inherent limitations imposed by the introductory format, and Hua is unable to incorporate recent studies or discoveries, or provide appendix material such as a map, glossary and bibliography. The translation is occasionally awkward or dubious, and insufficient editing further hinders the presentation. The extensive use of colour images introduces the reader to some of the most iconic images of historical Chinese dress, but these are unorganized and incompletely captioned, and there is no attempt to correlate text and image.

Despite these problems in editing and organization that will limit the book's impact, *Chinese Dress* succeeds in providing a flavour of the fascinating history and present-day issues in Chinese dress studies, and will be of great interest to textile and design students, professionals and collectors.

RACHEL SILBERSTEIN
University of Oxford

Grace Evans, *Fashion in Focus 1600–2009: Treasures from the Olive Matthews Collection* (Chertsey Museum, 2011). 152 pp., *c.* 170 illus. £11.99. ISBN 978-0-9568135-0-3.

Olive Matthews was, together with Doris Langley Moore and the Doctors Cunnington, one of the great twentieth-century collectors of historic dress in Britain. Like her contemporaries, her collection became the foundation of a nationally significant dress collection housed within a museum: Surrey's Chertsey Museum. (The collections of Langley Moore and the Cunningtons are housed at the Fashion Museum, Bath and the Gallery of Costume, Platt Hall, Manchester respectively.) Unlike her contemporaries, she wrote little about her collecting and collection, and little has been written about them save for a rudimentary museum booklet in 1976 and Valerie Cumming's tantalizing insight in her 2005 *Understanding Fashion History*. This imbalance has thankfully been redressed in Grace Evans' book, *Fashion in Focus 1600–2009*.

The introduction explores Olive Matthews' fascination with dress and her motivations for collecting. Her interest was for what she termed 'the antique' (referring to dress pre-1850) since 'styles I have known and worn I don't care about'. When she died in 1979, aged ninety-two, she left a collection of over 3,000 items of men and women's dress. Over the last thirty years, the collection has grown in both size and scope and now includes objects outside her original collecting remit. The earliest object is a Jacobean nightcap, bought by

Through detailed descriptions of these fashions and, more importantly, the dramatic changes in the fashionable silhouette, Evans provides a fascinating insight into the move from the Edwardian era to modern dress. The compensation claims made by some of the ladies after the disaster list the astonishing cost of such luxury and put into perspective the subsequent descriptions of the second- and third-class clothing. Many of these passengers hoped to begin a new life in America and in preparation for the journey had brought good, practical tailored outfits and money for their onward passage. Sadly, a high proportion of second- and third-class passengers (and children) who perished in the tragedy were subsequently identified by their dress.

In her final chapter, Evans details the uniforms of the servants, crew and other workers on board the vessel, giving a poignant insight into the sheer hard work involved in sailing the huge ship, highlighting the extreme contrasts between the dress of the privileged classes with their poorer counterparts. The sinking of *Titanic* was a pivotal event in the twentieth century, and hidden beneath an unprepossessing book cover lies an eloquently written, beautifully illustrated and well-researched social history which can be enjoyed by both dress and *Titanic* enthusiasts alike.

ELISE TAYLOR
National Museums Northern Ireland

Christine Boydell, *Horrockses Fashions Off-the-Peg Style in the '40s and '50s* (London: V&A Publishing, 2010). 192 pp., 180 col. illus. Hbk £24.99. ISBN 978 1 85177 601 6.

Few fashion styles sum up the British look in the 1950s quite so neatly as the printed cotton summer frock. And the name that every woman wanted was a crisp cotton Horrockses number, brightly coloured, distinctively patterned, and always looking fresh. These were the dresses produced by Horrockses Fashions, established in 1946 by the Lancashire cotton manufacturer Horrockses Crewdson and Company Ltd of Preston, founded in 1791.

The story of Horrockses Fashions is told in a new, richly illustrated authoritative book by Christine Boydell, produced by V&A Publishing. This is a wonderful source of information not only about this particular firm but also about both the British ready-to-wear industry in the 1940s and 1950s and post-war British society. It will appeal to those who have some familiarity with fashions of the time, as well as to a new generation of fashionistas. Christine Boydell has made a lifetime study of Horrockses, organizing two exhibitions around the subject: *Our Best Dresses: The Story of Horrockses Fashions* for the Harris Museum and Art Gallery, Preston, in 2001, and *Horrockses Fashions* at the Fashion and Textile Museum, London, in 2011. She shares her exhaustive knowledge about the firm in an attractive and accessible way in this interesting book.

The book examines key aspects that made the firm unique in four main chapters. There are sections, for example, on the importance of textile design (from prints by Alastair Morton and artist-designed textiles by names like Graham Sutherland and Edward Paolozzi to talented in-house women designers Joyce Badrocke and Pat Albeck), and also sections on promoting the Horrockses Fashions brand, as well as on retail and purchasing. There are details too of Royal patronage of the firm; both The Queen and Princess Margaret wore Horrockses cotton dresses in the 1940s and 1950s.

Throughout the book there is a wealth of photographic material, including colour images of surviving dresses from the collections of the Harris Museum and Art Gallery in Preston, Manchester City Art Galleries and the Victoria and Albert Museum in London (plus sumptuous details of the textiles) to contemporary publicity and advertising photographs, film stills and personal photographs. The book also has a useful set of references, including a monetary note on comparative values, a list of archive and museum collections with Horrockses-related material, and a select bibliography.

Horrocks summer dress from
*Horrockses Fashions Off-the-Peg Style
in the '40s and '50s.*

Part of the charm of this publication is the inclusion of so many personal photographs.
If you want to know what life really looked like in the 1950s, then the images in this book
are a delight: there is Greta Hetherington on a trip to London in 1955, or the Horrockses
Fashions' staff on a day out in Sussex, or on the river in the early 1950s. All are wearing
their Horrockses printed cotton frocks but surely with a knitted 'cardi' or wool coat to hand,
just in case the weather turned chilly.

*Horrockses Fashions Off-the-Peg Style in the '40s and '50s,* just like the Horrockses dresses
in their day, is a must-have buy, for this is a wonderful book about a fascinating area of
British fashion history and of British cultural life.

ROSEMARY HARDEN
The Fashion Museum, Bath

*Global Denim,* ed. by Daniel Miller and Sophie Woodward (Oxford: Berg, 2011). 204 pp.
b/w photographs and line drawings. £19.99. ISBN paper 978 1 84788 61 6; e ISBN 978
84788 739 9.

The two editors of this collection of essays by a wide variety of authors come from a background of material culture studies, both sociological and anthropological, and the approach
to the book, and indeed the Global Denim Project on which it is based, is an ethnographic
rather than an historical one. This is not to say that some of the essays do not look at
the historical background and more traditional view of denim jeans as an American icon.

In fact, the first essay looks at precisely this in Sandra Curtis Comstock's essay on the transformation of jeans during the Great Depression from basic, very cheap workwear into something which came to represent all things American, and a part of American national identity. This aspect is also taken up by Bodil Birkebœk Olesen, in looking at the way in which their significance in materializing American values plays an important part when reusing, donating or simply wearing jeans at the office, and can be viewed in 'green' and socially ethical terms.

Other essays look more at the way in which different cultures have adopted and adapted the denim jean to make it their own everyday clothing of choice. Claire Wilkinson-Weber examines how Bollywood films used denim as a shorthand to demonstrate the social mobility and internationalism of their characters, both male and female actors wearing denim in situations and at periods when it most certainly was not the norm in Indian society. Daniel Miller's essay, 'The Limits of Jeans in Kannur, Kerala', also looks at the wearing of jeans as an indicator of increasing urbanization and modernization in a traditional culture, with age playing a very decisive part in style of dress. The author also makes some interesting points when comparing the differences in dress of the Muslim and Hindu populations of Kannur, and the local population's ambivalence towards the wearing of jeans in general.

Most of the remaining essays look at various aspects of jeans, fashion and sexualization, in particular of the female body. Mykene Mizrahi's detailed study of the phenomenon known as 'Brazilian jeans' is a much wider ethnographic study of the dress and 'Funk culture' of young women in Brazil, and in fact does not deal with denim at all, as the Brazilian jeans are made of 'Moletom stretch' fabric dyed to resemble denim. Roberto Sassatelli's 'Indigo Bodies: Fashion, Mirror Work and Sexual Identity in Milan' again looks at sexualization (or at least the expression of it) of the bodies of both men and women by wearing jeans. Sophie Woodward's 'Jeanealogies' looks at jeans and expressions of intimacy in the context of personal relationships and the different attitudes of three women towards the wearing of 'boyfriend's jeans', and makes interesting points about their attitudes to 'genuine' distressing of long-term wear, and multiple wearers and the 'inauthenticity' of pre-distressed jeans.

Much closer to the expected subject matter are the final two articles, one by Moritz Ege, looking at the particular style of 'Carrot-cut jeans' in Berlin and the other by Rosana Pinheiro-Machado on 'The jeans that don't fit: marketing cheap jeans in Brazil'. Both articles develop and challenge very particular points raised by the 'launch' article for the Global Denim Project by Miller and Woodward, published in the journal *Social Anthropology* in 2007.

The articles vary widely and yet are also connected, along with the others available on the Project website: http://www.ucl.ac.uk/global-denim-project/. This includes additional illustrations, and perhaps one of the weaknesses of the published volume is the standard of the illustrations used in the book. The Project is set to continue and develop, both in a special issue of *Textile* (2011) and also a more wide-ranging *Wiki*-style open source publication, which will perhaps be more suited to the Project than this style of publication, however interesting and varied.

CHRISTINE STEVENS
Robinson Library, Newcastle University

Susan Ingram and Katrina Sark, *Berliner Chic: A Locational History of Berlin Fashion* (Bristol and Chicago: Intellect, 2011). 232 pp., 59 b/w illus. £22.50. ISBN-13: 978 1 84150 432 2; ISBN-10: 978 1 84150 369 1.

Germany is one of the main exporters of fashion and textiles and has a long history of manufacturing ready-to-wear. Hugo Boss, Esprit and Escada are well-known fashion brands, and the expatriates Karl Lagerfeld, Juergen Teller and Heidi Klum are household names in the fashion world. However, apart from Jil Sander and possibly Wolfgang Joop, designers based in Germany are rarely known beyond the nation's borders. Irene Guenther's *Nazi Chic? Fashioning Women in the Third Reich* (Oxford: Berg Publishers, 2004) is an exception to the rule that German fashion rarely features in English-language publications.

Using as their leitmotif a statement made in 2004 by Berlin's mayor, Klaus Wowereit, that the city was 'poor, but sexy', Susan Ingram and Katrina Sark examine very diverse aspects of Berlin's fashion identity, and these are loosely grouped together under different headings.

In the first two chapters, the authors describe how dress and related objects have been collected and displayed in Berlin and evaluate recent academic discourse. Photography is the focus of the next chapter where such different practitioners as Heinrich Zille, Helmut Newton, F. C. Gundlach and Rico Puhlman are discussed. This chapter is best read with a computer at your side. High reproduction costs have prevented the inclusion of all but a few relevant examples.

Chapter four deals with the relation between Berlin's film and its fashion industries, and includes a long 'excursus' about the use of Berlin as backdrop in the dystopian science fiction films *Aeon Flux* (2005) and *Equilibrium* (2002). Music has shaped the image of Berlin, and its clubs still attract large numbers of travellers. The authors look at the transformational power of Berlin's Hansa Tonstudio on musicians and bands like David Bowie and U2, the importance of the soundtrack to the film *Run Lola Run* (1998) and a representation of the city's techno scene in *Berlin Calling* (2008).

In the last chapter the status quo is examined, including the various attempts to turn Berlin into a fashion capital. You could read this in conjunction with another publication on the city's fashion scene published last year: Christine Bierhals' *City Fashion Berlin* (Potsdam: Ullmann, 2011).

If you are looking for a factual account of the history of Berlin fashion, this book might not be for you. While its fragmentary nature can be frustrating, it also might aptly reflect Berlin's history. At times *Berliner Chic* seems to ask more questions than it answers, but it provides many incentives and sources to explore Berlin's fashion identity further.

BEATRICE BEHLEN
Museum of London

# Obituary

## Richard Rutt CBE
### 1925–2011

*Photograph reproduced by kind permission of the Diocese of Leicester*

Monsignor Richard Rutt, who died on 27 July 2011, was widely known as 'The Knitting Bishop'. This was, perhaps, a regrettable nickname as he was so much more in a long and outstanding life: wartime code-breaker, linguist, missionary, Anglican Bishop, Bard of the Gorsedd of Cornwall, pelargonium specialist and, in his final years, a Roman Catholic priest. However, to English-speaking knitters he is chiefly remembered for his *History of Hand Knitting* (London: Batsford, 1987), widely regarded as a definitive work on the subject. His research collection of books, journals, patterns and other material on knitting is now held at Winchester School of Art Library at the University of Southampton.

Cecil Richard Rutt was born in Bedfordshire in 1925 and went from school into the wartime Royal Navy. After demobilization in 1947 he trained for the Anglican priesthood, took a degree at Cambridge and volunteered for missionary service in Korea, where he was

DOI: 10.1179/174963012X13319136517430

to spend almost twenty years. He spoke at least eight languages and wrote widely on Korean culture and literature.

Richard Rutt had been taught to knit by his grandfather at the age of seven, and it is said that he sometimes resorted to this craft to relieve the tedium of meetings. After his return to Britain he knitted some of his own regalia, notably his golden mitre when he became Suffragan Bishop of St Germans in Cornwall. As Bishop of Leicester from 1979 to 1991, he found himself based in a historical centre of machine knitting. He was appointed CBE in 1973. When he retired to Cornwall with his wife Joan, an Early English specialist, he converted to Roman Catholicism and was ordained a priest. He was made a Prelate of Honour, with the title of Monsignor, by Pope Benedict XVI in 2009.

When the Early Knitting History Group (EKHG) was formed in 1993, Richard said he was thrilled by the 'fascination of knitting history' and he influenced and inspired our meetings with his lectures (a tough journey from Cornwall for someone in poor health). This enthusiasm illuminated his *History of Hand Knitting*, which was reviewed in *Costume*, 22 (1988). The reviewer, Donald King, wrote: 'Humane, lucid, and accurate, this is an excellent reference book, scrupulously presenting the historical facts, stripped of legendary accretions. Costume historians will find a great deal to interest them'. Inevitably, some of his book is now outdated, although it is still treasured, quoted and frequently referenced by students of the subject. Richard himself had hoped to revise it, particularly the Elizabethan section, after meeting Janet Arnold who was also interested in knitting (he admired her book *Queen Elizabeth's Wardrobe Unlock'd* and thought her 'perhaps the most distinguished costume historian of her generation').

As a '*quondam* bather' with back trouble, Richard took up swimming and in 1990 an article appeared in *Costume* (24) on 'The Englishman's Swimwear'. It is a serious, sixteen-page essay on a very small subject — men's swimming trunks, from nudity to aquadynamics. [Its importance is underlined by Jean Williams in her article in this present volume on 'Aquadynamics and the Athletocracy', in which she notes that the term aquadynamics, defined here as the technical development of sports clothing and its embodiment, was first used in *Costume* by Richard Rutt. Eds.]

Richard's interest in knitting, 'a people's craft', was based on years of research and practical work, but he wrote profusely on other subjects in three or four languages. In latter years he kept in touch through the Knitting History Forum (the reformed EKHG) and nice emails replaced nice letters. He wrote that his study was confined to books as he could not 'get around to look for things anymore'. Richard Rutt was very good company and will be remembered as a man of great personal charm.

KIRSTIE BUCKLAND

*Costume*, vol. 46, no. 2, 2012

# The Costume Society Awards

As a registered charity with a constitutional aim of providing education in dress studies, the Costume Society has five sources of funding to support this aim.

**The Patterns of Fashion Award** honours the work of the dress historian Janet Arnold (1932–1998), a founder member of the Society. An award of £500 is open to students studying on dress and fashion-related education courses that involve the design and realization of costume. It is awarded to the student who has, in the opinion of the judges, produced a *reconstructed* garment from a pattern in one of the Janet Arnold *Patterns of Fashion* books that reflects the high standards presented in the books.

**The Yarwood Award** commemorates the dress historian and former chairman of the Costume Society, Doreen Yarwood (1918–1999). The award is offered for a period of three academic years to an MA course in dress history or costume design at a specified academic institution. An award of £500 is made annually to one of its students whose final project or dissertation would benefit from research into the history of dress. It is intended to help the student with travel costs and any other expenses incurred during the course of this research. Accredited courses may apply to the Costume Society for consideration as future award holders.

**The Symposium Student Bursary** to attend the Costume Society's three-day symposium. It is open to UK full-time and part-time students at graduate and postgraduate level engaged in research directed towards the presentation of a dissertation or thesis. Ideally, the research should either reflect a theme of that year's symposium or be an object-based research project on the history of dress. The bursary offers full attendance at the symposium inclusive of accommodation, meals and all visits and activities in the symposium programme, but does not cover transport to and from the symposium. **This award is generously sponsored by Maney Publishing.**

**The Student Design Award** is an integral part of the Society's symposium and is not open to the public. A fashion course at an art school close to the symposium venue is asked to participate — with the cooperation of tutors to suit their tight course programmes. A design brief, based on the theme of the symposium, is set to encourage and inspire the students to visit local museums and galleries for their research work. The Student Design Award project culminates in a one-hour catwalk show during the symposium, when eight finalists are chosen to present their made garments and to discuss their designs, aims and inspiration. An award of £250 is presented to the winner.

**The Museum Placement Award** of up to £1,000 funds a student volunteer, for a minimum of two months, to work on a dress-related project in a public museum collection in the UK; applications are made jointly by a student and an appropriate museum. The award is intended to support students seeking work experience in this subject area and to help UK museums accomplish projects essential to the care, knowledge or interpretation of dress collections.

**Further information** on the terms and conditions, application procedures and contact details for these awards may be found on the Costume Society's website: **www.costumesociety.org.uk**

 DOI: 10.1179/174963012X13319136517476

# London Antique Textile Fair

Sunday 7th October 2012
10.30am to 4.30pm

Admission: £6
Concessions £4

Chelsea Old Town Hall
SW3 5EE

www.textilesociety.org.uk